PSYCHOLOGY

IN
100 QUOTES

METRO BOOKS
New York

An Imprint of Sterling Publishing Co., Inc.
1166 Avenue of the Americas
New York, NY 10036

ISBN 978-1-4351-6783-4

For information about custom editions, special sales, and premium
and corporate purchases, please contact Sterling Special Sales
at 800-805-5489 or specialsales@sterlingpublishing.com.

Manufactured in China

2 4 6 8 10 9 7 5 3 1

sterlingpublishing.com

Design by John Christopher

MIX
Paper from
responsible sources
FSC® C017606

PSYCHOLOGY

IN
100 QUOTES

ALEX
FRADERA

METRO BOOKS
New York

INTRODUCTION

Exploring the nature of the mind is one of humanity's oldest enterprises. Its roots are evident in the thinking of the earliest philosophers, and they probably run much farther back, too, given the evidence of mind-expanding drug use and ritual shamanic practice at that time. Our ability to read people's dispositions, figure out their states of mind, and reflect on our own feelings suggest that we are all, in our own ways, natural psychologists.

Modern psychology developed from the Enlightenment-era mission to understand our world without reliance on existing dogmas, putting the mysterious into a legible system or to the scientific test. It gathered shape in the 18th century and became a distinctive field in the following one, thanks largely to a focus on measurement and replication, which was developed in Germany's experimental tradition. This was imported to North America by the pioneering thinker William James, where it quickly gathered its own momentum. Informed by the work of the Russian Ivan Pavlov, Americans such as John Watson developed an approach to psychological science that dominated the first half of the 20th century: behaviorism. Advances in the field, notably from French and British scientists, led to the new science of psychometrics—the study of human variation in mental ability and other traits. This was psychology as the domain of the measurable.

Meanwhile, Sigmund Freud's psychoanalytic approach was seeking to dredge the deepest interiors of the mind. A new profession was created, the therapist, which remains the main type of psychologist that people come into contact with. Therapies have since proliferated, inspired by philosophies ranging from the pessimistic to the fervently hopeful, from the straightforward to the esoteric.

In the modern era, psychological science entered new epochs; cognitive psychology addressed the operations of the mind, and social psychology the individual's relationship to the wider group. The latter is notable for having captured the public imagination through a slew of often controversial experiments, as researchers sought to understand difficult political and moral problems, such as authoritarianism.

When considering the mind, the matter of the brain is never too far away. Psychiatrists investigating neurological disease, neuroscientists mapping brain activity to mental tasks, and evolutionary psychologists looking for biological reasons our minds developed as they did have all contributed to the story of psychology. By interlacing with existing fields, psychologists form new ones, leading to spirited debate about what exactly "mind" is.

This book will take you along the waterways of psychology, along its major branches, through some colorful backwaters, and into uncharted territories. The journey will take in some views that may be controversial, and inclusion in the book should not be read as an endorsement. Where possible I have indicated when a topic is heavily contested, but the best approach is to read beyond these snapshots. The psychological community has recognized that its scientific practices are far from watertight, and one result is that a number of exciting and well-established psychological phenomena are now sunk or sinking. This is addressed directly in various sections but has also contributed to decisions on what not to cover.

One hundred quotes are insufficient to do justice to all the figures who have contributed to psychology and all the fascinating phenomena they have illuminated. However, this book explores some of the subject's most important issues, through the words of its most significant thinkers.

Men are disturbed, not by things, but by the principles and notions which they form concerning things.

EPICTETUS
ca. 55–ca. 135 CE

SOURCE: *Enchiridion*
DATE: ca. 135 CE
FIELD: Therapy

The Stoic school of thought, founded by the philosopher Zeno in 3rd-century Athens, stressed that the only good or bad in life is what we bring to it. The external features of existence are just opportunities to act virtuously—to be prudent with a fortune won, courageous with an injury endured—but we must move past destructive self-centered emotions to do so. This is summed up in our quote from the Stoic Epictetus, and it is a view of life that has proven to be influential. This is because Epictetus' observation have also informed the modern way we treat psychological problems, thanks to an individual named Albert Ellis.

A shy youth, Albert Ellis trained himself at nineteen years old to be more confident by approaching and speaking to 100 women in one month, desensitizing himself to rejection. In this we see the glimmerings of the philosophy he formalized in the 1950s as rational emotive behavioral therapy (REBT). Rather than the psychoanalytic approach of diving into childhood experiences or the unconscious, this therapy addressed faulty thoughts and beliefs by acting on them directly. In the following decade, Aaron Beck—with whom Ellis had been corresponding—identified a series of cognitive distortions that cause psychological problems, and over time REBT and other methods became aspects of a new approach to therapy developed by Ellis and Beck: cognitive behavioral therapy (CBT).

Stoic thinking is at the heart of CBT. It declares that a major source of our suffering is in the way we interpret our circumstances. It follows that we can alleviate our suffering by challenging the interpretation. Thanks to its systematic and reproducible methods, CBT has built up a large evidence base and is now a primary way of treating mental health issues.

SINCE THE WORLD CAN IN NO WAY SATISFY OUR CRAVINGS,

LET US LOOSEN OUR HAIR TOMORROW AND GO FISHING

02

LI PO
701–762

SOURCE: *The Penguin Book of Chinese Verse*
DATE: 8th century
FIELD: Well-being

Psychological science grew initially from a Western paradigm, but in recent years it has developed through insights expressed in Eastern religion, philosophy, and art. The exquisite verse opposite comes from Li Po, a Szechwan poet considered one of the greatest of his period. An irreverent and zesty individual, he lived as both wanderer and court poet. His writing shows the influence of Daoism and chimes with today's psychology.

"The world can in no way satisfy our cravings": We now understand how one of our major brain reward systems, the dopaminergic system, supplies good feelings as we get closer to a goal—but once we have achieved it, the system dies down. Finally we get the accolade we always wanted, but then what?

The Daoist philosopher Zhuangzi suggested that the solution is not to seek goals. He presents a parable in which the Chinese philosopher Confucius is surpassed by his student, who announces, "I just sit and forget." Psychology research is now discovering the profound effect of sitting meditation practices, whereby you allow yourself to shed attachment to worldly experience. Worries, concerns—how real are they right now? Do we choose to take on these burdens and treat them as real? Zhuangzi wrote: "May I suggest that goodwill and duty do not belong to the essentials of man?" When we recognize that effortful questing will never end in peace, we can turn to the peace that was always, effortlessly there. Let us loosen our hair tomorrow and go fishing.

Reason is, and ought only to be the slave of the passions, and can never pretend to any other office than to serve and obey them.

03

DAVID HUME
1711–1766

SOURCE: *A Treatise on Human Nature*
DATE: 1739
FIELD: Emotion

Growing up in a distinguished but cash-strapped family, David Hume was forced to earn a living, but he found he could give his attention to nothing but the world of the intellect. Although his dedication brought him to the verge of a breakdown, we are all beneficiaries: At age 28, he produced *A Treatise of Human Nature*, considered one of the greatest works in philosophy. He explicitly used the tools of natural science to investigate human psychology, looking at motivation and morality. Modern cognitive scientists have described the book as their founding document.

The quote opposite illustrates Hume's belief—in contrast to the Greek rationalist tradition (see page 7)—that our lives, and the basis of our morality, are inevitably rooted in feeling. When we feel that something is good, it signals a virtue, and bad signals a vice. Many psychologists have rejected this view; Lawrence Kohlberg advocates a theory in which rationality is the "moral force" that develops in stages to produce more sophisticated moral conduct. However, in recent years the psychologist Jonathan Haidt has defended the Humean perspective. His research shows that when people moralize on issues, they like to emphasize their concern about the harmful consequences—you shouldn't kill a dog, because it deprives the dog of life. Yet when presented with scenarios where no harm is involved, such as eating one's dead pet dog, people betray their true emotions—it's wrong because it feels wrong. We may not want to celebrate this, but we should be aware of it. Our evolved emotions have a commanding hold on our sense of how the world should be.

The only thing necessary for the triumph of evil is for good men to do nothing.

04

EDMUND BURKE
1729–1797

SOURCE: Unknown
DATE: 18th century
FIELD: Social psychology

This quote is attributed to 18th-century Irish philosopher Edmund Burke, although it is possibly apocryphal. It expresses his belief that a society depends on its members being virtuous in practice, not just in their own minds. Examples of such failure fascinate psychologists, none more than the events of March 13, 1964. This was the night that Kitty Genovese was raped and murdered in a New York residential neighborhood. The papers reported how—despite repeated cries for help—no neighbor intervened or called the police. We now know this account of apathy was exaggerated. The furor at that time did, however, spur psychologists John Darley and Bibb Latané to investigate what they called the bystander effect.

When is someone less likely to help a victim? When they are one bystander among many. This robust effect has a few causes: When in public, we obey social norms by keeping to ourselves, rather than putting our antennae up and outward. One bystander study pumped smoke into a waiting room; it was noticed by a solitary person within a fraction of the time it took a group. Yet a bigger factor is diffusion of responsibility. If someone else could help, why should I? If they don't, doesn't that suggest that it's acceptable not to? The effect is hard to shake, but it is lessened when bystanders identify with the victim, and bucked by people who are more extroverted and have a sense of responsibility to the world at large. It's easy to hide in a crowd, but what kind of world do we want to live in?

The same remedy will produce more beneficial effects when prescribed by a **famous** physician, than by a person of inferior character.

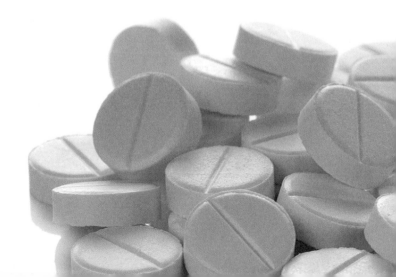

05

JOHN HAYGARTH
1740–1827

SOURCE: *Of the Imagination, as a Cause and as a Cure of Disorders of the Body*
DATE: 1800
FIELD: Suggestion

The British physician John Haygarth helped to reduce diseases like smallpox and typhus through the introduction of health prevention techniques, such as inoculation and quarantine. His contribution to psychology was to debunk a contemporary fad, the Perkins tractor. Proponents claimed these instruments, basically pointy-ended metal rods, could draw out all sorts of disease. Haygarth demolished these claims by showing that sham wooden versions of the tractor were as effective as the real ones. The cure was entirely due to the expectations of the individual. As he wrote, this showed, "To a degree which has never been suspected, what powerful influence upon diseases is produced by mere imagination"—whether this be an exotic device or the reputation of the doctor. He had discovered the placebo effect.

Some people have found a silver lining in the existence of placebo. These optimists suggest that at least part of it reflects something interesting: Mental expectations can improve mental, or even physical, well-being. Placebo pessimists point out that much or sometimes all of the effect is less exciting—a patient tells the doctor what they want to hear, or their natural recovery from illness is misattributed to the medication or treatment they received. Thus, placebo studies shouldn't be used as evidence of mental self-healing; any such evidence has to come from more focused research. What is incontrovertible is that the placebo effect is a complication for any medical research, a fly in the ointment of investigating treatment. You have to account for the human factor.

**Anxiety
is the
dizziness
of freedom.**

06

SØREN KIERKEGAARD
1813–1855

SOURCE: *The Concept of Anxiety*
DATE: 1844
FIELD: Existentialism

Visitors to 1830s Copenhagen might have witnessed a strange figure constantly walking its crooked streets: a gawky youth with his hair crested six inches above his forehead. That youth was Søren Kierkegaard, and behind the forehead thoughts crackled and wrestled, producing the ideas that would make him the father of existential philosophy. Kierkegaard's key preoccupation was choice, reflected in the title of his magnum opus, *Enten/Eller* (*Either/Or*). As humans, we are blessed—or cursed—with the ability to choose, and Kierkegaard explored how the problem of choice could explain that uncomfortable mental state. *Either/Or* begins with the image of someone standing at a cliff edge, considering a leap to his death.

The man may feel a focused (and logical) fear of falling, Kierkegaard writes, but also a wider-ranging emotion—"angst," translated as anxiety or dread—at the sense that he could choose to jump at any moment. This is the dizziness of freedom. A modern psychiatrist might not address anxiety from this existential angle, but they would maintain Kierkegaard's distinction between a pathological phobia focused on a specific object, like spiders or needles, and a more generalized anxiety, which largely revolves around whether we have met, or will meet, the challenges posed to us by existence. For Kierkegaard, anxiety was not necessarily bad; it was a reminder to us not to be complacent, to never forget that we get to be an agent in the world. A life entirely without anxiety would be one without possibility. This is the existentialist challenge: to manage your anxiety, make your choices, and live by the path you've chosen.

I am no bird; and no net ensnares me; I am a free human being with an independent will.

07

CHARLOTTE BRONTË
1816–1855

SOURCE: *Jane Eyre*
DATE: 1847
FIELD: Literature

At a time when women were socially subordinated, Charlotte Brontë and her sisters managed nonetheless to become celebrated novelists. Concealing their gender under pen names, their writing changed 19th-century Britain by exposing it to unheard feminine perspectives. In this quotation, Brontë uses her character Jane Eyre to express an attitude to life that she undoubtedly lived by. Psychologists have explored this idea too, through something called self-determination theory. Proposed by Edward Deci and Richard Ryan, it aims to understand motivation. What propels us to act, to constructively participate in the world? The answer: when acting is an end in itself, and when we experience intrinsic motivation.

Intrinsic motivation is found in activities in which we can see ourselves improving and gaining mastery over the challenge. It's found in activities in which we deepen our relationships with other people. Above all, it's found in activities we ourselves choose to do. We elude the snaring nets and choose to make more of ourselves, and of our ties to those around us.

Intrinsic motivation is why many people find volunteering so rewarding. It illustrates why external incentives can be insufficient, even counterproductive. Studies show that, under some conditions, paying people to complete a task makes them less intrinsically motivated. The choice to continue is now less free ("Think of the money!"), so the task becomes a means to an end, not an end in itself. This is not to say that people should not be compensated for work, and fairly, but mastery, relation, and freedom appear the enduring sources of human motivation.

By the term Hypnotism [...] I mean a peculiar condition of the nervous system [...] which differs, in several respects, from common sleep or the waking condition.

08

JAMES BRAID
1795–1860

SOURCE: *Observations on Trance or Human Hibernation*
DATE: 1850
FIELD: Perceptions and biases

James Braid was a Scottish surgeon involved in improving the treatment of clubfoot and other conditions. In his spare time, he became fascinated with a craze, then known as mesmerism or animal magnetism, in which charismatic figures claimed to heal people using their gaze. This phenomenon began in the 18th century with the physician Franz Mesmer, who believed he had cured a patient of hysteria by feeding her an iron-laced preparation and then attaching magnets to her. Mesmer later became convinced that he himself was the agent, transmitting a *lebensmagnetismus* (invisible natural force) that overwhelmed the patient. Braid was a gentleman scientist in his spare time, and after reading skeptical reports decided to see for himself at a series of magnetism demonstrations in Manchester, England.

The trances he witnessed were convincing, but Braid wondered: Does this really require the work of an external force? Braid began experimenting by putting himself into a trance and found he could do so by concentrating his attention in what he called the "upwards and inwards squint." He then showed that the technique worked on others. These demonstrations debunked the magnetism account, while showing that the phenomenon—which he preferred to call hypnotism—was real.

To Braid, hypnosis was a condition similar to but distinct from sleep, and one "solely attributable to a peculiar physiological state of the brain"—an account that science has continued to broadly support. Even with his attempts to demystify hypnotism, Braid took some flak at the time. Today, Braid is simply remembered as the father of modern hypnotism.

Try to pose for yourself this task:
not to think of **a polar bear**, and
you will see that the cursed thing will
come to mind **every minute**.

FYODOR DOSTOEVSKY
1821–1881

SOURCE: The essay "Winter Notes on Summer Impressions"
DATE: 1863
FIELD: Cognitive psychology

The Russian novelist Fyodor Dostoevsky is often considered the most successful explorer of human psychology through fiction. Among his discourses on innocence, criminality, ethics, and ideology, he made the observation quoted opposite, which made a great impression on the late Harvard professor Daniel Wegner. "I was really taken with it. It seemed so true." So in 1987 Wegner decided to test it, asking research participants to spend five minutes talking about whatever came to mind, while trying not to think of a white bear. This proved no easy feat, with participants thinking of the pale ursine an average of once a minute. This experiment was the basis of Wegner's "ironic process" theory—the idea that it's hard to deliberately *not* put your attention somewhere.

The reason for this is that, by forbidding a thought, a mental routine is set up to monitor for that thought, which sensitizes the mind to the very thing that it wants to push away. This has had implications for clinical treatment. For instance, trying to block out the idea of a cigarette may make things harder for a quitter. It may also be one component of reoccurring thoughts, in anxiety-related ruminations, and in the devastating post-traumatic stress disorder (PTSD).

If you want to manage unwelcome thoughts, Wegner proposed a few tips: Focus actively on something else, or allocate some time when you're prepared to think through the issue so it bothers you less later. Make a mental visit to a blue ocean, or visit that bear properly, during zoo opening hours.

EVERYONE

KNOWS

WHAT

ATTENTION

IS.

WILLIAM JAMES
1842–1910

SOURCE: *Principles of Psychology*
DATE: 1890
FIELD: Existentialism

Born into an intellectually brilliant family, which included his novelist brother Henry, William James may have had the deepest mind of all. On a visit to Germany he experienced the burgeoning science of physiological psychology. Returning to Harvard, he began teaching these concepts. He went on to contribute lasting ideas on the nature of emotion, habits, free will, and religious experience, including personal experimentation with psychotropic substances, such as amyl nitrate and peyote.

Previous thinkers had thought that life experience simply falls upon us like raindrops on a roof. James had no truck with this passive, reactive view of the human being; he was certain that our minds had purpose and agency. Moreover, this view of humans as experience sponges doesn't match with reality. For example, consider how, at a noisy party, an engrossing conversation makes all the hubbub drain away. In James' words, "My experience is what I agree to attend to. Only those items which I notice shape my mind—without selective interest, experience is an utter chaos." He observed that conscious multitasking is therefore a fiction: At best, we switch between different objects of attention, which is less efficient than focusing on just one.

The extremely open-minded James founded the American Society for Psychical Research, and contributed to pragmatic philosophy, insisting that truth is ultimately what works. He thought that reality can never be held steady and looked at objectively; rather, by shining our beam of attention here or there, we create our own individual reality.

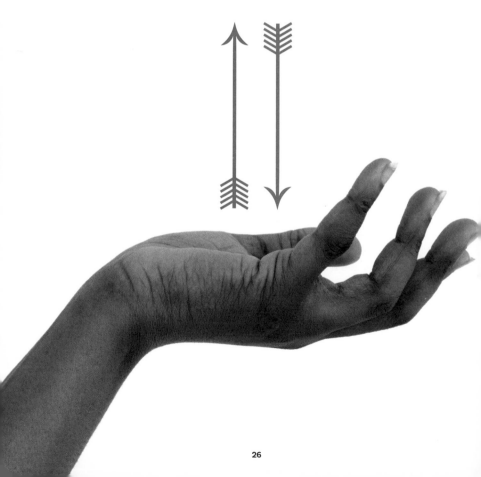

Our mental life
has grown up
as a mediation
between stimulus
and reaction.

EDWARD THORNDIKE
1874-1949

SOURCE: *Animal Intelligence*
DATE: 1898
FIELD: Behaviorism

To understand Edward Thorndike, start with a box. Thorndike's puzzle box was a small wooden affair holding an animal, typically a cat, that wanted out. When the cat triggered a lever the door popped open, and Thorndike measured how long it took his subject to make its escape. The animal was then returned to the box for another go, and Thorndike once again timed its escape. By graphing the times, Thorndike showed that there was no feline "eureka" moment; the improvement in escape times was gradual—literally, a learning curve. This suggested the cat was mainly using trial and error, but increasingly focusing its actions to those made when it had succeeded in the past. This became his "law of effect": Actions that produce good results are likely to be repeated in the future. Stimulus causes reaction.

Thorndike collected data on animals and humans during his long tenure at Columbia University. He showed how improvements in learning are incremental and automatic—keep throwing darts and you will gradually improve, although you may struggle to say why. His data also showed that associations used recently become stronger and more flexible, while those left in disuse become weaker. Thorndike was passionate about applying his insights to education. His law of effect states that learning depends on positive feedback, so he advocated praise for behaviors that we want to encourage and ignoring those we do not. His focus on measuring behavior paved the way for an approach that dominated psychology well into the middle of the 20th century.

Dreams are the royal road to the unconscious.

12

SIGMUND FREUD
1856–1939

SOURCE: *The Interpretation of Dreams*
DATE: 1899
FIELD: Psychoanalysis

Sigmund Freud was a medic, theorist, and world-shaker. In his view, humanity's comforting sense of self had already been rocked by "two great outrages": Copernicus overturning the theory that the earth is the center of the universe; and Darwin toppling man from his specially created position as separate from the animal kingdom. Freud saw himself at the forefront of a third outrage; empirical evidence of psychology had proved that the individual "is not master in his own house."

An uneasy participant in high-class Viennese society, thanks in part to his Jewish background, Freud used his outsider eye to search unrelentingly for hidden and ugly truths sitting below the rational surface of his seemingly respectable patients. He worked using hypnosis, before developing his technique of free association, encouraging patients to make uncensored responses to the words he gave by volleying another one back without premeditation. Prince among his approaches was dream analysis, which he saw as a way to access issues that the unconscious needed to articulate but were too taboo to be expressed directly.

Through this data, Freud developed a theory of the psyche as a tussle between sub-personalities—the impulsive, sensation-seeking id of our animal past; the moralizing superego representing social forces; and the balancing, organizing ego. He believed that "rather than living our lives, we are 'lived' by unknown and uncontrollable forces." Psychoanalysis, the study of the psyche, became a major approach to tackling psychological problems. Although Freud's specific view of the psyche is unpopular with modern researchers of the mind, the idea of nonconscious forces governing our behavior is now firmly established.

'This child will never achieve anything […] He is not intelligent at all.' I have heard such rash statements too often.

13

ALFRED BINET
1857–1911

SOURCE: *Modern Ideas about Children*
DATE: 1909
FIELD: Psychometrics

The French psychologist Alfred Binet was the architect of the first practical intelligence test, the Binet–Simon test. It was revolutionary, and it has shaped our approach to schooling, job recruitment, and clinical diagnosis. Yet Binet's original aim was modest and undeniably humane: to identify children with learning disabilities, so as to provide them with support. He and his research student, Théodore Simon, developed the test to predict a child's mental age from their responses to items that ranged from simple sentence repetition to abductive reasoning challenges, like "My neighbor has been receiving strange visitors. He has received in turn a doctor, a lawyer, and then a priest. What is taking place?"

As this quote suggests, Binet was not a harsh determinist who viewed test results as destiny. He believed intelligence varied from situation to situation and was influenced by the environment. In his view, intelligence was too subtle to ever fully capture in quantitative (scored) methods. An ideological view of intelligence hardened thanks to American proponents of eugenics, who saw mental testing as a way to promote white supremacy, something that horrified Binet when it was brought to his attention.

The latest research concurs, stating that while there is a strong heritable component to general intelligence, an individual's intellectual prowess is also influenced by life conditions. Intelligence testing is still used to diagnose learning difficulties, the progression of dementia, and the consequences of head injury. It's no surprise that the Binet–Simon test features in the top twenty greatest scientific developments of the century in the journal *Science*.

Careful and **exact** measurement does not reveal a periodic mental or motor inefficiency in normal women.

LETA STETTER HOLLINGWORTH
1886–1939

SOURCE: "Functional Periodicity"
DATE: 1914
FIELD: Perceptions and biases

Leta Hollingworth fought uphill. At a young age she and her siblings were tugged from their grandparents' Nebraska farm to the "fiery furnace" of life in their alcoholic father's household. Her gender was an obstacle to progression in a number of fields: writing, despite being published in her local paper at 15; teaching, due to state by-laws preventing mothers from doing so; and for a time she found no route into graduate school. She lived at a time when it was accepted that women were weaker than men, both physically and mentally, and lacked powers of judgment and rationality. It's no surprise that once she could finally begin research, Hollingworth waged war on these ideas. In her PhD thesis, she attacked the folk belief that menstruation impairs women's capacity to perceive, act, or think clearly. Over three months, she meticulously recorded and measured performance by women on tasks requiring accurate thinking, perception, or action, and found that their capability did not depend on the menstrual cycle. The folk belief was mere prejudice. Hollingworth argued that a woman's influence on society was not confined by her limitations, but by society's.

Her passion for justice extended beyond issues of gender. She investigated how the new intelligence test was being used to identify mentally defective children, discovering that the test was misdiagnosing individuals who were actually suffering from emotional difficulties. Later in life her passion for education led her to pursue the betterment of gifted children. "The Evolution of Common Things" was her empowering system of learning, whereby children developed their own ways of understanding features of their everyday lives, such as food, clothing, and communication.

We live trapped,
between the churned-
up and examined past
and a future that
waits for our work.

15

ANNA FREUD
1895–1982

SOURCE: Reprinted prose piece in *Anna Freud: A Biography* by
Elizabeth Young-Bruehl
DATE: 1920
FIELD: Therapy

Anna Freud was the youngest daughter of Sigmund, the founder of
psychoanalysis. She became a practitioner and theorist of the approach,
which was concerned with exposing troubled undercurrents of thought, and
she made a major contribution to the application of analysis to children.
Her own childhood was challenging; a distant mother, difficult relations with
her siblings, and likely depression and eating disorders no doubt informed her
own work.

Around the time of this quote, Anna Freud had already begun what became
almost a decade of periodic analysis with her father, after a bout of tuberculosis
had interrupted a budding teaching career. She dedicated herself instead to
exploring the mind, in particular her father's concept of the ego, the mediating
force between animal appetites and suffocating social structures.

Her work identified five defense mechanisms used by the ego to cope with the
anxieties created by the threat of forbidden feelings making an appearance,
including the repression of unacceptable feelings, the projection of these
feelings onto others, and their sublimation. This last one is the healthiest
mechanism, whereby the individual expresses the feeling appropriately.
Minimizing the ego's use of the other, counterproductive mechanisms is part of
the psychoanalysts job. To the end, Anna Freud worked to defend and extend
the legacy of her father, committed to the idea that the core concern of therapy
was the conflicts within.

He feels solitary, indescribably unhappy [...] He has a feeling as if something has cracked in him.

16

EMIL KRAEPELIN
1856–1926

SOURCE: "Manic-Depressive Insanity and Paranoia"
DATE: 1921
FIELD: Psychiatry

In this quote, the German psychiatrist Emil Kraepelin describes manic depression, a disorder he identified by digging deeper into what was then a catch-all diagnosis of "psychosis." In Kraepelin's time, psychiatry was new and somewhat unrefined: A single obvious symptom was often the basis upon which diagnosis of mental ill-health was made. Yet this tended to lump together patients who behaved and responded very differently. Just as a physician would not rush to a diagnosis based on a fever, Kraepelin insisted on deemphasizing individual symptoms. Instead, he focused on the *syndrome*, the pattern of symptoms and their development over time. This focus helped him recognize that psychosis was (at least) two entities: "dementia praecox," which we now know as schizophrenia; and manic depression, which subsequent researchers separated further into bipolar disorder and major depression. His lab also made great progress in the analysis of diseased brain tissue—together with Alois Alzheimer, he is credited with the discovery of Alzheimer's disease.

Kraepelin's medical and scientific beliefs spilled out into his social views. He assumed repeated criminality was due to degeneration of brain tissue— a psychiatric explanation for the idea that some people are "born criminal." Like many contemporaries, he was a eugenicist who deplored what he saw as the weakening of the gene pool. Yet he protested against the conditions of contemporary asylums, seeing madness as an illness to be treated, not a crime to be punished. Modern psychiatry, and its core text, the *Diagnostic and Statistical Manual of Mental Disorders*, focuses on mental syndromes and their biological causes. We are following the tracks Kraepelin laid down almost a century ago.

WHAT CAN THIS BE?

UNIDENTIFIED REVIEW OF THE TEST OF HERMANN RORSCHACH
1884-1922

SOURCE: *Journal of Nervous & Mental Disease*
DATE: 1921
FIELD: Therapy

Hermann Rorschach gained the nickname Klecks as a child due to his hobby of klecksography, using inkblots to make pictures. Although artistic, Rorschach decided to pursue a scientific career and studied psychiatry under the distinguished Eugen Bleuler (who also tutored Carl Jung). Rorschach was interested in the new field of psychoanalysis, where free association of words revealed hidden meanings. It reminded him of his childhood inkblots, which would be interpreted differently by different viewers. If words could trigger secret truths, why not images?

Rorschach presented hundreds of inkblots to his patients, and winnowed them down to ten that were both evocative and ambiguous. In 1921, he published them, together with their instructions, in the dense *Psychodiagnostik*. In the years that followed, others popularized the test, which was initially intended only to diagnose schizophrenia but was then expanded into a test of personality—an application about which Rorschach had been skeptical.

The test involves looking at the image and making gut associations, before a second round of closer examination is conducted, during which subtle actions, such as whether the patient rotates the page, are taken as further data to assess personality. The test is nowadays out of favor, thanks to questions over its validity and whether the associations are too well-known, but it is still in use by some therapists. In pop culture, it keeps popping up, from Andy Warhol to Alan Moore's *Watchmen* superhero saga.

GIVE ME A DOZEN HEALTHY INFANTS [...] AND I'LL GUARANTEE TO TAKE ANY ONE AT RANDOM AND TRAIN HIM TO BECOME ANY TYPE OF SPECIALIST.

18

JOHN B. WATSON
1878-1958

SOURCE: *Behaviorism*
DATE: 1924
FIELD: Behaviorism

In 1913, John B. Watson marshaled the spirit of a new force in psychology and spoke its name. He had turned to studying people after a spell researching animal behavior, in the tradition of Ivan Pavlov (see page 43). Believing that the rigorous principles of animal research were superior to current methods in human research, he published a manifesto, "Psychology as the behaviorist views it." In it, he argued psychology should limit its investigation to observable behavior, because consciousness is too elusive to study scientifically, writing, "introspection forms no essential part of its methods." The domain of animal research had also shown how behavior was produced by learned associations, which he believed could one day explain all of psychology.

The quote opposite from Watson should be understood as part of an ongoing debate. He worked in an age of advocates of a fixed human nature and outright eugenicists. Watson defied that status quo in a deliberately provocative manner, going on to say, "I am going beyond my facts and I admit it." Still, he fully believed that the bulk of human variety was due to learning and the environment. This wasn't merely theoretical talk; Watson and his research assistant Rosalie Rayner later married and put the Watsonian doctrine into practice in their child-rearing. They treated their children as small adults, believing sentimentality in parenting produced invalidism and false expectations for how the world will treat them: their how-to book *Psychological Care of Infant and Child* stated, "Mother love is a dangerous instrument." Rayner expressed later ambivalence in her article "I am a Mother of Behaviorist Sons," and sadly one of their sons committed suicide at the age of 40. Today, Watson is remembered for being in the vanguard of this new science, and for his bold manifesto.

The different kinds of habits based on training, education, and discipline of any sort are nothing but a long chain of conditioned reflexes.

19

IVAN P. PAVLOV
1849-1936

SOURCE: "Conditioned Reflexes: An Investigation of the Physiological Activity of the Cerebral Cortex"
DATE: 1927
FIELD: Behaviorism

When Russian physiologist Ivan Petrovich Pavlov won a Nobel Prize in 1904, it was a case of fourth time lucky. The award was for work on "the physiology of digestion," which doesn't sound psychological. However, by training dogs to salivate on cue, he was unlocking why we behave as we do. Pavlov called saliva a "psychic secretion," arguing that is produced automatically at the mere expectation of food. His investigations showed that this automatic response could be grafted onto other events that occurred simultaneous to the arrival of food. By repeatedly pairing the food with a bell or tone, he established that the sound alone will prompt salivation. This Pavlovian, or classical, conditioning can be seen in many parts of life, like the ex-smoker suddenly craving a cigarette when walking past his favorite bar.

This idea that behavior is the result of learned associations was a seed that grew into the powerful behaviorist school of psychology. Fiction writers have been horrified and fascinated by conditioning and its potential for social control, as seen in novels like *Brave New World* and *A Clockwork Orange*. Meanwhile, Pavlov had actually lived within a repressive regime, Soviet Russia. It lauded his genius, but he did not respond in kind; he was a vocal critic of how it treated its citizens, making statements and even writing critical letters to Stalin himself. Despite this, he managed to live a long life. Today, he and his ubiquitous dogs symbolize the basic building blocks of our behavior.

The feelings and desires of a baby
know no limits, since they are
a part of everything he SEES,
TOUCHES, and PERCEIVES.

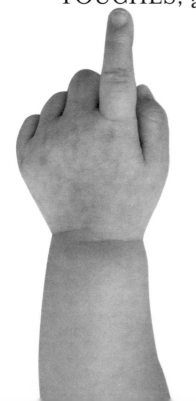

20

JEAN PIAGET
1896–1980

SOURCE: "The First Year of Life of the Child"
DATE: 1927
FIELD: Child development

The Swiss psychologist Jean Piaget made many contributions to his field, but his best known comes from a discovery early in his career. He was struck by the mistakes the youngest children made on the new Binet–Simon intelligence test (see page 31). The systematic pattern suggested to him that the children were seeing the world in a fundamentally different way. When they became older, they left these errors behind, as they acquired a more sophisticated but still incomplete worldview. This is Piaget's well-validated theory of the stages of child development.

At the earliest age, which is described in this quote, the baby has begun the sensorimotor stage, characterized by reflexive action and no real sense of "I" versus "the world." Gradually the baby comes to see itself as separate, and at around two enters a new stage where it can treat objects symbolically—the child hands you a banana, so you can make a phone call. Still, they struggle to see things from other people's point of view. It is at later stages that the child begins to reason logically and grasp the laws of physical conservation, such as knowing that a volume of liquid poured from a wide glass into a slender one remains the same, even though the liquid now reaches a higher level.

According to Piaget, transitions are the result of work done by children themselves, who are always collecting and testing data against their current understanding. At some point, unexplainable data builds up to break the banks of the old theory and the child sees the world anew. They've leveled up.

 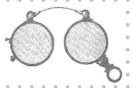

Memories [...] are actually mental reconstructions that are coloured by cultural attitudes and personal habits, rather than being direct recollections of observations made at the time.

FREDERICK BARTLETT
1886–1969

SOURCE: *Remembering*
DATE: 1932
FIELD: Memory

Bartlett was a British psychologist who investigated how thinking is influenced by our culture and assumptions. He is best known for his memory research, especially his examination of how a story changes through its retelling. The "War of the Ghosts" originates in a Canadian First Nations culture. It tells of a young man invited by mysterious warriors to join a raiding party. He is injured, despite feeling no pain, then later abruptly dies. It's an unfamiliar narrative to a Western audience, and Bartlett was curious how British participants would keep the details straight. His first participant read the original story and described everything they could remember. Next, a transcript of their words fed the next participant, beginning a chain of retelling like a game of Telephone.

The distortions that emerged revealed the storyteller's cultural assumptions. Facts crucial to the original culture seemed irrelevant to the Westerners, such as the subtle reference to the titular ghosts, which soon disappeared. The death scene detail, "Something black came out of his mouth," was transformed over repetitions into the Christianized "his spirit left the world." Other details were Westernized: "bush cat" became "cat"; and "paddling in canoes" became "rowing in boats." Bartlett concluded that we simplify the world using sets of assumptions, or schemas, that help us put incoming information into a familiar context. As essential as these schemas are, they make us prone to misunderstanding events that don't follow the script. Memory—indeed, the human mind—likes to normalize, to standardize, to smooth over the strange.

Human nature is almost unbelievably malleable.

22

MARGARET MEAD
1901–1978

SOURCE: *Sex and Temperament in Three Primitive Societies*
DATE: 1935
FIELD: Human universals

Margaret Mead was a leader in the field of anthropology, but her efforts reverberate through psychology, specifically the debate over whether people are shaped mainly by biology or society—the power of nature versus nurture. In her fieldwork in the South Pacific and Asia she explored cultural norms, particularly those of sex and sexuality. Having grown up in an America that she found stifling and repressive, she believed that documenting a worldwide variety of ways of life could open up the same possibilities at home. In *Coming of Age in Samoa*, Mead described a permissive society where premarital sex occurred without sanction and largely free of sexual jealousy. In her later work she documented nonpatriarchal and mainly pacifistic societies in Papua New Guinea, which was considered an intellectual foundation for the burgeoning feminist movement. Her observations also influenced the celebrity pediatrician Benjamin Spock, and through him a generation or more of Western parents absorbed her recommendations about breastfeeding on demand.

Mead's work had a political component, was politically influential, and inevitably provoked political resistance. Her research has been labeled poor and even unscientific by some. The most serious allegations, of naivety and myth-making, have largely been disproved, although it's also clear that Mead downplayed aspects of Samoan society that didn't fit with her expectations. The Papua New Guinea findings on pacifism may also be anomalous, influenced by the Australian administration in Papua New Guinea banning warfare before Mead began her studies. Patriarchal societies seem more ubiquitous throughout humanity's existence than Mead had hoped. However, her work was successful in inspiring many to ask: What could be possible now?

$$B = f(P, E)$$

23

KURT LEWIN
1890–1947

SOURCE: *Principles of Topological Psychology*
DATE: 1936
FIELD: Social psychology

Since Wilhelm Wundt's *Principles of Physiological Psychology* declared psychology "a new domain of science" in 1874, it has sought laws and equations to prove its credentials as a science. There were notable early examples, particularly from the German school, such as Hermann Ebbinghaus' forgetting curves, or Gustav Fechner's law on detecting small changes in a sensory stimulus. Yet the road to psychology being acknowledged as a valid branch of the sciences has been bumpy, and this goal might never be achieved.

Kurt Lewin's elegant equation, opposite, is not a mathematical formula, but an invitation to think harder about how people intersect with the world around them. Lewin, German-born but later naturalized in the USA, had an eclectic research career that spanned many aspects of psychology, including the behavioral, social, and organizational. He had a knack for drawing insights from everyday events: His theory of motivation involving the building up of psychic tension was inspired by a restaurant visit, during which he observed how his waiter behaved over the course of the meal.

A rich thinker, thanks in part to his fascination with the complexities of the real world, he was dissatisfied with the binary argument over whether environment or individual forces were the determinants of human behavior. His experience as a Jew in Germany during the rise of Nazism had made evident the power of external forces. Yet he did not he view the individual as passive. Rather, behavior (B) was a function or product of the person (P) and their environment (E). Thanks to this insight, Lewin explored and founded a research center for a wholly new approach to behavior—the study of group dynamics—and shaped the direction of social psychology.

To what extent do
we know that the results of
intelligence tests given by
white examiners to Negro
children are reliable?

24

HERMAN GEORGE CANADY
1901–1970

SOURCE: "The Effect of 'Rapport' on the IQ: A New Approach to the Problem of Racial Psychology"
DATE: 1936
FIELD: Psychometrics

African Americans weren't getting the best treatment from the psychologists of the 1930s, and Herman George Canady marshaled his energy to change that. African-American himself, he campaigned to improve psychology training at black colleges and raised questions about how well the predominantly white field was capturing the black experience. In "The Effect of 'Rapport' on the IQ," Canady addressed the issue of an examiner's race on psychological testing.

Given the racially stratified society in the USA, it seemed possible that test results would be skewed by unconscious bias or test-taker anxiety. He ran an experiment in which white and black children completed IQ tests, administered once by a white examiner and on another occasion a black one. Canady's analysis showed that when tested by an examiner of the same race, both black and white children scored about six points more than on their other attempt. As IQ scores can fluctuate on retest to this degree, Canady refused to draw absolute conclusions, but he did recommended that the testing environment be taken seriously. Additionally, he was laying the groundwork for others to explore. In the last twenty years psychologists have explored how tests are affected by stereotype threat, an anxiety produced by reminders that people of your group are not expected to perform well. Canady's cultural factors put sand into the gears of objective measurement.

KNOWING YOUR
OWN DARKNESS
IS THE BEST METHOD
FOR DEALING WITH
THE DARKNESSES
OF OTHER PEOPLE.

CARL JUNG
1875–1961

SOURCE: *Letters of C. G. Jung: Volume I*
DATE: 1937
FIELD: Therapy

For a time, Sigmund Freud saw the Swiss psychiatrist Carl Jung as his long-awaited "crown prince and successor." The older Freud had developed psychoanalysis, an approach to mental health treatment focused on unconscious desires, and he saw the brilliant younger man as worthy to carry the flame. However, the spiritually minded Jung parted with his atheistic mentor. For him, the unconscious contained much more than Freud's mainly sexual preoccupations. He believed it held ancestral experiences, collective memory compressed into archetypal concepts such as the Hero, which we could draw on to make sense of ourselves. Although he agreed with Freud that humanity had a dark side, he saw potential in that darkness. "Everyone carries a shadow," he wrote, "and the less it is embodied in the individual's conscious life, the blacker and denser it is." By facing and incorporating the shadow, we access power we have mistakenly denied and progress toward being whole.

Some of the ideas Jung developed, such as the constructs of extraversion and introversion to describe personality, have taken root in the scientific soil. Others are less at home there. As well as the aforementioned collective unconscious, he believed in synchronicity, the idea that events that coincide but have no causal relationship can nevertheless be treated as connected and meaningful. As much mystic as scientist, Jung's impact is perhaps clearest in terms of his ideas on mythological archetypes, which have influenced countless stories. His therapeutic approach, analytic psychology, continues to be popular among the creative and story-minded.

Give me the doll that looks like a colored child.

26

MAMIE PHIPPS CLARK / KENNETH B. CLARK
1917–1983 / 1914–2005

SOURCE: "Racial Identification and Preference in Negro Children"
DATE: 1947
FIELD: Identity

Playing a decisive role in the civil rights movement is something few
psychologists can claim. That accolade is, however, owed to Mamie Phipps
Clark and Kenneth B. Clark, who demonstrated the emotional and
psychological damage done to African-American children by a segregated
society. Phipps Clark had witnessed small victories while working for a civil
rights lawyer in the District of Columbia. Convinced of the possibility of
change, she conducted her Master's degree research on "The Development of
Consciousness of Self in Negro Pre-School Children." Her husband Clark's
interest was piqued, and he joined her to develop the work into their now-
classic doll experiments.

They presented African-American children with two dolls, one fair-skinned
and blonde, the other with black hair and dark skin. The children were asked
their opinions: Which doll has nicer hair? Which would you prefer to play
with? Which is the bad doll? In the majority of cases, the white doll was judged
more favorably, and the black one rejected. Phipps and Clark then asked the
children to identify which doll resembled them better. This frequently upset
the children, who became agitated or even stormed out of the room.

During the Brown versus Board of Education of Topeka proceedings on the
constitutionality of segregated schools, the psychologist pair gave testimony on
their studies. When segregation was struck down, this testimony was one factor
cited as influencing the decision. Afterward, the pair went on to found and run
a community center in Harlem, providing help for poor black children and
continuing to study the effects of racial bias.

It is a mistake to suppose that the whole issue is how to free man. The issue is to improve the way in which he is **controlled.**

27

B. F. SKINNER
1904–1990

SOURCE: *Walden Two*
DATE: 1948
FIELD: Behaviorism

Behavioral psychologists before Burrhus F. Skinner had agreed that scientists shouldn't explain behaviors by referring to thoughts, because they were too tricky to measure and quantify. Skinner's radical behaviorism went further. He considered thoughts to be just another kind of behavior, of no real difference to a flinch or increase in salivation. He didn't want to set aside the mental realm; he wanted to explain it away entirely. Like Edward Thorndike before him (see page 27), Skinner studied animals under controlled conditions.

His meticulous work integrated two lines of research: Pavlov's classical conditioning, whereby an automatic response (salivation at the sight of food) is transferred to another stimulus, such as a bell ringing; and Thorndike's research on pay-offs and punishments that influence future behavior, called instrumental conditioning. Skinner believed conditioning could explain almost everything, from superstitious behavior to language. In his view, organisms are ultimately mechanical and our actions and thoughts are products of chains of cause and effect. His model allowed no space for mental agency.

Skinner's greatest legacy has been in determining how habits are made or broken through different programs of reinforcement. He showed that when a behavior triggers rewards, but intermittently and unpredictably, it is very hard to eliminate the compulsion to try the behavior again—a principle that explains both the addictive nature of gambling and our need to check social media, experiences crafted by behaviorism-savvy companies. In this sense, we live in a post-Skinner world, and when we reflexively reach for our phone when it pings, we should reflect on who exactly is in control.

There is in every child at every
stage a new miracle of vigorous
u n f o l d i n g .

28

ERIK ERIKSON
1902–1994

SOURCE: *Childhood and Society*
DATE: 1950
FIELD: Therapy

Who was Erik Erikson? He was German who became American; he was a
Christian, but first he was a Jew. Erikson was a name he created for himself,
and he was in some ways a self-created man. He lived through what there had
been no name for—a crisis of identity—but he was to change that.

Erikson was encouraged into psychoanalysis by Anna Freud (see page 35),
whom he worked with at a school and who noticed his rapport with children.
After gaining his qualification, he conducted fieldwork with native tribes, such
as the Oglala Sioux, where he observed psychological problems unconnected to
the sexual issues focused on by psychoanalysis. These were individuals who,
after their way of life had been demolished, were struggling to find themselves.
They were uprooted and alienated.

Erikson realized the concept of identity fell in psychotherapy's blind spot, and
he devoted himself to illuminating it, both in healthy development and in
crisis. His research suggested identity should develop by stages across a person's
lifespan, in a model often called the Eight Ages of Man. Each age reveals more
of the whole person, while bringing its own challenges. For example, only
when you are old enough to grasp that you can achieve things for yourself—and
be a person with initiative—is it possible for you to fall short of this possibility,
and thus experience guilt. According to Erikson, it's tasting both the new
potential and the failure to reach it that allows identity to develop—meaning it
isn't easy, but it is crucial.

The great majority of us cannot listen; we find ourselves compelled to evaluate, because listening is too dangerous.

29

CARL ROGERS
1902–1987

SOURCE: The article "Communication: Its Blocking and Its Facilitation"
DATE: 1952
FIELD: Therapy

Second only to Sigmund Freud in influence as a psychological clinician, Carl Rogers developed an approach steeped in humility. His person-centered therapy rejected the assumption that the client is a passive set of problems for the expert to cure. The therapist's duty was to offer people an opportunity to grow.

How? Above all, listen. Rogers believed listening was rare and often came with criticism. He insisted on listening with "unconditional positive regard," making no judgment of the person's basic worth, whatever they revealed. Every person was the best expert on themselves, and this was an opportunity for them to speak out and reveal their truth. Without it, they would flee toward ideal, impossible versions of themselves, ideals that harmed them by distorting their perceptions and denying parts of themselves. Turning from the ideal to the real wasn't easy, but Rogers maintained it was the way forward to growth. "The curious paradox is that when I accept myself just as I am, then I can change."

This listening-centered approach is also a road to settling arguments. Rogers recommended going no further in a dispute until you can restate the other person's position to their satisfaction, thus bridging the gap of misunderstanding and proceeding from the clearest possible perspective. In his final years, Rogers traveled widely, using the techniques he had developed to help groups reconcile their differences in countries such as Northern Ireland, apartheid South Africa, and post-dictatorship Brazil.

A
musician
must make music,
an artist must paint, a
poet must write, if he is to
be ultimately at peace with himself.
What a man can be, he must be.

30

ABRAHAM MASLOW
1908–1970

SOURCE: *Motivation and Personality*
DATE: 1954
FIELD: Existentialism

Born into a working-class New York neighborhood, Abraham Maslow was
a timid, bookish youth. He was hassled by anti-Semitic gangs and found
interacting with peers a struggle. He felt there was more he could offer the
world, but this had to wait while he focused on staying safe and being liked.
These first-hand observations led Maslow to his idea of a hierarchy of needs,
often represented as a pyramid, with physiological needs at the base (water,
warmth), and safety, love, esteem, and self-actualization farther up.

Maslow believed that until lower needs are met, they tend to monopolize our
attention. The more they are settled, the more we can devote ourselves to
higher levels, including self-actualization: being what we can be. Maslow
documented traits of people he considered self-actualized, including accounts
of figures like Albert Einstein and Jane Addams. They were self-accepting and
comfortable being alone, they dealt effectively with their problems, and they
had deeper relationships. To Maslow, these were elements of a desirable human
psychology that deserved to be given more attention. "It is as if Freud supplied
us the sick half of psychology and we must now fill it out with the healthy half."

Maslow's humanistic approach to psychology was future- and growth-focused,
and spoke the language of personal responsibility. It influenced therapy and
self-help theorists, including an entire 1960s movement promoting self-
actualization. His work anticipated the positive psychology movement, and he
began the investigation of "peak experiences," such as mystical, ecstatic states of
awe and connection, directly inspiring the field of transpersonal psychology
that aims to make sense of spiritual experience.

THAT REASONABLY INTELLIGENT AND
WELL-MEANING YOUNG PEOPLE ARE
WILLING TO CALL WHITE BLACK IS A
MATTER OF CONCERN.

31

SOLOMON ASCH
1907–1996

SOURCE: "Opinions and Social Pressure"
DATE: 1955
FIELD: Perceptions and biases

As a young child one Passover night, Solomon Asch was curious about the extra glass of wine. It's for Elijah—the protecting prophet—came the reply. Wow—would he really take a sip? Yes, his uncle assured him: Watch the level of the wine go down. The young Asch watched... and thought he saw something. As an adult and research psychologist, Asch wondered if he had actually been fooled by the power of social pressure.

In his conformity experiments, groups of participants were involved in an apparently simple task: Say which of three straight lines matches the length of a fourth. The answers were given out loud, and what the last participant to speak didn't know is that the rest were secret collaborators, who started colluding to give obviously wrong answers. In response, participants would frequently conform to the majority response; only a quarter always stuck to the clearly correct answer. As few as three collaborators were sufficient to produce the full conformity effect. To get people to state obvious falsehoods, you don't need the mantle of emperor, just a few buddies to back you up.

Asch believed conformity was a power akin to hypnotism, with a huge influence in shaping society—people run with the herd. It's an effect exploited by marketers: "Millions love our product, so you'd be crazy not to." However, conformity founded on lies is fragile. In a variant study where one collaborator spoke out against the false consensus, Asch's participants almost always joined the revolt. Just like the boy from the story, be prepared to shout loud when the emperor has no clothes.

TO BE HUMAN MEANS TO FEEL INFERIOR.

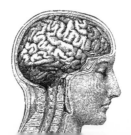

ALFRED ADLER
1870–1937

SOURCE: *The Individual Psychology of Alfred Adler: A Systematic Presentation in Selections from His Writing*
DATE: 1956
FIELD: Therapy

Week after week, the young doctor Alfred Adler would meet in Vienna with a coterie of thinkers who went on to shape the development of psychology. This was Sigmund Freud's Wednesday Society, the seed of the psychoanalytic movement. Before long, animosity with Freud led to a split, with Adler taking his followers to a new approach, individual psychology.

Adler thought Freud's focus on the unconscious past neglected the social realm: the forces of control, power, and motivation that shape our behavior. What of the need for control, our striving for perfection? Life, it seems, imposes a sense of inferiority on us at every opportunity. Mindful of this, Adler jettisoned the analyst's couch—at least during therapy, we could attempt to be two equals sitting together. His ideas became popular, due in large part to his optimistic and straightforward approach. One apocryphal story tells of a patient reporting to Adler his family history, woes, and symptoms. Adler asked what he would do, if he got cured. After the answer, Adler replied, "Well, go and do it then."

Adler was a socialist, social idealist, and feminist, opposed to systems that cultivated and accentuated inferiority. He encouraged families to be more democratic, letting their children participate and have a say in their futures. He also recommended practical action to his patients, that they actively cooperate with others in their lives to better their collective conditions. Today Adler's philosophy is in use both in individual psychology and its influence on cognitive behavioral therapy.

7±2

MY PROBLEM IS THAT
I HAVE BEEN PERSECUTED
BY AN INTEGER.

33

GEORGE A. MILLER
1920-2012

SOURCE: The article "The Magical Number Seven, Plus or Minus Two: Some Limits on Our Capacity for Processing Information"
DATE: 1956
FIELD: Cognitive psychology

Born in West Virginia, George Armitage Miller started his research career at Harvard in a secret World War II project to jam signals for the US Army Signals Corp. As the focus of his work shifted to speech and hearing, he started to observe an effect he had noticed elsewhere, centered on the number seven. When asked to identify the tone they had just heard, or the line they saw flashed onscreen, people struggled when there were many more than seven options. When people were asked to hold a list of letters in their head, they struggled once the list exceeded seven characters in length.

Miller figured there must be a numerical limit to what we can pay attention to. At that time, psychological science was dominated by one approach, behaviorism, which focused on observable actions and considered the hidden workings of the mind as too unscientific to study. Yet Miller had always been interested in the mind, and his new proposal made sense of what were vexing mysteries. For example, counting large numbers of items occurs one-at-a-time, but smaller sets, of seven items or fewer, we can do in a flash (an ability called subitizing). One behavior, counting, with two different mental processes at work.

With colleague Jerome Bruner, Miller founded the Center of Cognitive Science. Miller saw the word cognitive as "an act of defiance" that introduced a new field: cognitive psychology, the study of the mind. For this, and his spooky number seven, Steven Pinker placed him "among the most influential experimental psychologists of the 20th century."

Colorless
green
ideas sleep
furiously.

34

NOAM CHOMSKY
b. 1928

SOURCE: *Syntactic Structures*
DATE: 1957
FIELD: Language

Noam Chomsky is known worldwide as one of the intellectual leaders of the radical left. Before that, however, he made waves in academia by launching a new paradigm for linguistics, one which challenged the tenets of psychology.

Read the quote again; it's curious. It is a statement without intelligible meaning, but it nonetheless reads like a sentence. This was a problem for the still-dominant psychological approach of behaviorism (see page 59), which claimed that language is simply a series of learned associations—the words "brown" and "dog" were paired repeatedly with a brown dog until all became connected. In this way, simply through the pairing of vocal sounds with objects in the world, language can be explained without investigating the inner mind. Yet in what world would "colorless" be paired with "green," or "green" with "ideas"? Yet the sentence holds some sense, and that's because of grammar.

Chomsky made a compelling argument that the extent of our mastery of grammar, the structuring of language, is far greater than can be accounted for by learned association. The mapping from reality to language is impossible to build from scratch. There must be something sitting under the hood—a protogrammar, waiting from birth for confirmation of how verbs or adjectives work in this particular language. He called this a "universal grammar." Since Chomsky, this idea has been hugely influential, though it remains controversial (see page 127). However, the case he stated for it was powerful enough to undermine the theory of behaviorism. The hidden structures of the mind might be baffling, but psychology could ignore them no longer.

Déjà Vu All Over Again.

35

YOGI BERRA
1925–2015

SOURCE: *What Time Is It? You Mean Now?: Advice for Life from the Zennest Master of Them All*
DATE: Reportedly 1961
FIELD: Cognitive psychology

The baseball catcher and coach Yogi Berra is a sporting legend who won more World Series than anyone in history. Off the field, he was famous for his "Yogi-isms": aphorisms with a paradoxical and (deceptively) innocent quality, such as, "I didn't say everything I said." In this quote, Berra deftly captures the essence of *déjà vu*—the sense that a current experience has happened before.

Déjà vu is not uncommon—around two-thirds of us have experienced it—and from the 1960s there was a sensory explanation as to why. According to this theory, in rare instances information received by both our eyes fails to arrive at our brain's visual centers simultaneously, meaning we experience the same event twice in very rapid succession. However, researcher Akira O'Connor put paid to that idea in 2006 by demonstrating that blind people can also experience déjà vu in response to sounds and smells.

The best current explanation is that déjà vu is due to a glitch in our memory systems. A current event awakens a memory, but incompletely, giving us a strong sense of familiarity without any specifics on which to pin it. The experience has a few relatives: *presque vu*, the sense that you are about to have an epiphany; and *jamais vu*, where normally familiar things become weird—something you can reproduce for yourself by repeating a word over and over again. Such conditions can be distressing when they arise persistently in psychiatric illness, but for most of us they're just curious flickers in our experience of the world.

Grapes are sourest
when they are in easy reach.

36

LEON FESTINGER
1919-1989

SOURCE: *Cognitive Dissonance*
DATE: 1962
FIELD: Decision-making

Brooklyn-born Leon Festinger, one of the most cited psychologists of the last century, reconceived our understanding of self-deception. He once infiltrated a doomsday cult and found they became even more fervent believers once their scheduled apocalypse failed to show. This contributed to his concept of "cognitive dissonance"—the discomfort that comes when you notice you hold contradictory ideas that motivate you to shift one or other.

To test this, Festinger created situations in which people acted against their own beliefs for tenuous reasons. He and his colleague James Carlsmith asked people to complete monotonous tasks, like rotating dozens of wooden pegs. They were then asked to tell the next participant it was enjoyable, either for a decent payment or a pittance. Those paid well later privately rated the task as boring, which it was. Those paid poorly rated the task as more enjoyable, to remove the dissonant notion they would lie for no real reason.

Later, Carlsmith took this idea to experiments with children, leaving them in a room of toys but taking a favored one out of bounds. In cases where the toy was physically removed, the child remained effusive about the taboo toy. When the toy was left in the room, and the child given only a mild sanction to stay away, their interest soured. After all, if the consequences were minor, why would they have forgone the chance to play with a truly great toy in easy reach? Festinger's idea shows you don't need to be a cultist to delude yourself.

FOR A SCIENCE FAIR AT MY SCHOOL, TWO FRIENDS AND I CONDUCTED A CONTROLLED EXPERIMENT TO SEE HOW LONG I COULD STAY AWAKE.

37

RANDY GARDNER
b. 1949

SOURCE: The television show *To Tell the Truth*
DATE: 1964
FIELD: Well-being

Of all the wild teenage schemes, it's hard to beat the one Randy Gardner decided on in 1963. The 17-year-old set out to win the local science fair by setting a world record for voluntary sleep deprivation. Two friends kept vigil in shifts, later joined by a sleep researcher, who verified the herculean—or somnambular—effort: 264 hours (11 days) without sleep. For this he won his 15 minutes of fame.

Sleep is a mystery we are still unlocking. Not all animals do it, and the sleeping body burns almost as much energy as a waking one. So what is it for? Certainly, our mental well-being. In an NPR interview, Gardner said, "It was crazy, where you couldn't remember things, it was almost like an early Alzheimer's thing brought on by lack of sleep." Research confirms that sleep deprivation interrupts memory—particularly memory consolidation, the passing of daily experiences into long-term storage, which relies on many stages of the sleep cycle. In addition, lack of sleep can disrupt language, planning, and time perception, and tips us into habitual behaviors like mindless eating. Slumber is needed for our brain to tend to itself.

We snub this at our peril. Later in life, Gardner experienced brutal insomnia that lasted for years. We cannot know if this is related to his record-breaking effort, as Gardner believes, but it is a reminder to take care. Sleep debt accumulates, and over the long-term our odds of depression and anxiety rise as we neglect the soft embrace of the duvet.

The effects of 6 months of total social isolation were so devastating and debilitating [...] 12 months of isolation almost obliterated the animals socially.

HARRY HARLOW
1905–1981

SOURCE: The article "Total Social Isolation in Monkeys"
DATE: 1965
FIELD: Child development

Pits of despair. Iron maidens. Rape racks. These aren't props for a horror movie, but Harry Harlow's macabre terms for his research equipment. During animal learning experiments, Harlow had noticed odd behavior in young monkeys raised apart from their parents. Seeing resonances with the ongoing debate on whether caregiver contact mattered to human babies (see page 109) he decided to investigate himself.

Harlow paired infant monkeys with surrogate monkey mothers fashioned from wire and wood. The maturing infants often developed digestion problems, which Harlow put down to lack of "contact comfort." Monkeys would cling to a surrogate, decked out in soft material, preferring it to a bare wire surrogate, even when the latter held the only food source in the cage. Convinced of his work's significance, Harlow began extreme experiments on social deprivation.

He housed monkeys for years in an isolation chamber—the pit of despair— where they could see and smell, but never interact with others. These monkeys would pace in circles, stare blankly, or even mutilate themselves. Next, the well of despair, where no light or sound could enter. Six months proved extremely damaging, and two years led to "autistic self-clutching and rocking"—one monkey even starved itself to death on release. (For insight on his other devices we suggest you research at your discretion.) Harlow justified his actions thus: "If my work will save one million human children, I can't get overly concerned about ten monkeys." Yet his grotesque lexicon gives away the game: This well-intentioned work was not merely a road to hell, but its worldly incarnation. His experiments helped provoke the animal liberation movement and greater ethics in animal research.

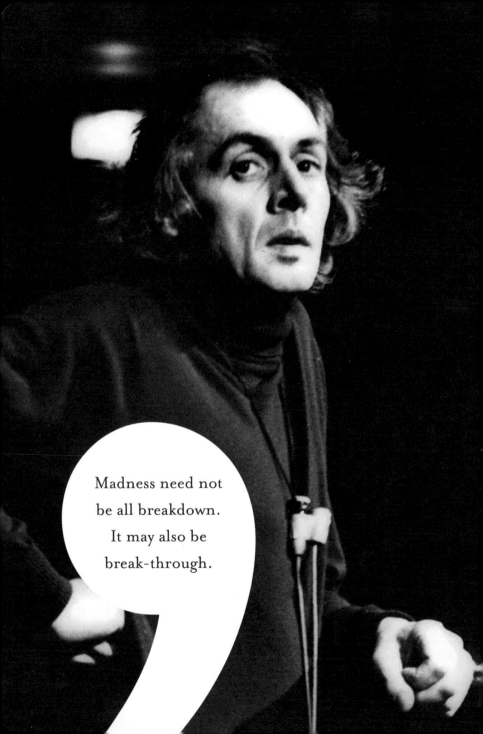

Madness need not
be all breakdown.
It may also be
break-through.

39

R. D. LAING
1927–1989

SOURCE: *The Politics of Experience/The Bird of Paradise*
DATE: 1967
FIELD: Psychiatry

The psychiatrist Ronald. D. Laing was never inclined to toe the line. The Glaswegian was a precocious, talented medical student who was not shy of criticizing shortcomings in the hospital powers that be, a habit he believed led to him being failed on his first attempt to gain his qualifications. As a newly qualified psychiatrist he would spend his downtime between appointments in corridors and waiting rooms, chatting with his (often schizophrenic) patients rather than his peers. By closing the gap between doctor and patient, he found they had far more in common than he had imagined.

Laing came to believe that clinicians were putting up barriers—professional distance, diagnosis, and medical language—that kept them from understanding their patients' predicaments. It was easy to categorize and pathologize symptoms like confusion and flights of fancy—even though we all experience them from time to time. However, this can miss how these experiences may be significant in themselves—the acting-out of real-life challenges that needed expression and resolving. We were medicating these symptoms away, whereas Laing decided to honor and explore them.

Laing is a key figure in the antipsychiatry movement—along with Thomas Szasz, who considered Laing insufficiently committed because he would still participate in treatment. The more extreme Szasz refused to participate, believing that "In the past, men created witches: now they create mental patients." Laing, however, believed that whether or not a diagnosis was real, the patient was in genuine distress and deserved attention that the psychiatrist could provide—the right kind of attention, such as meeting the patient on common ground, considering them individuals instead of members of categories, and relating to them as humans in friendship.

THE PSYCHOLOGY OF WOMEN HAS HITHERTO BEEN CONSIDERED ONLY FROM THE POINT OF VIEW OF MEN.

40

KAREN HORNEY
1885–1952

SOURCE: *Feminine Psychology*
DATE: 1967
FIELD: Therapy

Karen Horney derived a great deal of benefit from the psychoanalytic theories of Sigmund Freud, when therapy had helped her during a punishing year in which she became a mother and lost both parents. After she had gained her qualification in psychotherapy, however, she was quick to diagnose the problems in this very male-led tradition.

In *Feminine Psychology*, she unpacks a number of assumptions that are as naive as those of a young boy about girls. Boys assume that girls have a penis, and when they learn otherwise, see them as a "castrated, mutilated boy"; psychoanalysts diagnosed women as having a castration complex. Boys see girls as inferior for missing a penis. Analysts see girls as feeling inferior due to "penis envy." As she comments with admirable understatement, this should at least make us think.

Instead of focusing on the male sexual organ, perhaps male dominance in society might be a useful place to understand women's psychological issues? Consigned to the role of wife, Horney argued, women had to be objects of charm and beauty; as mother, to live to please others, rather than finding their own true purpose. Overall the relationship between the sexes had been deformed into one more like a parent and disempowered child. This is fertile ground to search for the basis of neurosis.

In a lovely touch, she turned the tables on Freud. What, she asked, explained the restless male energy that insists on projecting itself onto the world? What drove the need for success, for invention, constructing buildings, and amassing wealth? This curious, unquenchable need for visible creations had to be compensating for something, Horney mused. So perhaps it's simply a matter of "womb envy."

When, over time, the actions of another group appear to threaten a cherished goal of his group, the individual joins with enthusiasm into the formulation and execution of aggressive plans.

MUZAFER SHERIF / CAROLYN WOOD SHERIF
1906-1988 / 1922-1982

SOURCE: The article "Motivation and Intergroup Aggression: A Persistent Problem in Levels of Analysis"
DATE: 1970
FIELD: Social psychology

During his early life in Turkey, Turkish-American psychologist Muzafer Sherif witnessed ethnic conflict and was imprisoned for opposing fascism, experiences that impressed upon him how groups can commit terrible acts.

Together with his wife Carolyn, who met him while a high-achieving graduate student at Princeton, he devoted his life to exploring intergroup conflict. Together they conducted the Robber's Cave experiment. Around a dozen boys of age 11–12 gathered for two weeks of adventure at an Oklahoma summer camp. The boys created a pecking order, a group name—"The Rattlers"—and traditions like "Rattlers don't complain."

Then it was revealed there was another group of boys on the territory. Enmity developed, heightened in baseball games and tugs of war. The presence of rivals only deepened loyalty to the in-group: however they are, we should be different. For instance, the unnamed group dubbed themselves the Eagles, a creature formidable enough to eat rattlesnakes. The situation escalated: Cabins were raided, flags were burned, and rocks and weapons were collected.

This cavalier treatment of the children would be unacceptable in modern psychology. Not that this was not the first attempt: The Sherifs abandoned an earlier run where the groups flatly refused to turn against one another. Yet even that is significant. The kids met before the experiment and had already begun forming a group, and their adversary became the meddling experimenters. This set of studies showcases what has become one of the most robust findings of social psychology: Group identity is strengthened by the presence of an out-group, which can propel the group to efforts good and bad.

THE MIND IS A FORMIDABLE JAILER.

42

PHILIP ZIMBARDO
b. 1933

SOURCE: "A Pirandellian Prison," *New York Times Magazine*
DATE: 1973
FIELD: Social psychology

In 1971, soon after accepting a professorship at Stanford University, Philip Zimbardo embarked on one of psychology's most infamous studies. He installed himself as superintendent of a mock prison, assigning student volunteers as prisoners or guards for the next two weeks. The guards quickly took to their roles, mandating physical exercise as punishments and dealing with resistors by stripping them and putting them in solitary confinement. Prisoners became passive and depressed, and the experiment was halted after six days over concern for their welfare.

Zimbardo concluded that people are quick to develop cruel and authoritarian methods when given the chance, a tendency enhanced by conformity and anonymity, as with the guard uniforms and whistles. Meanwhile after early resistance the prisoners fell into their roles; even in downtime only discussing prison issues and their powerlessness, as if they had forgotten their very different life of only days before. They became prisoners, just as the guards became guards, trapped by their own social roles and mindset. Zimbardo later stepped into the Abu Ghraib prisoner scandal to emphasize the power of these roles: Don't pin it on the bad apples, look at the bigger picture.

Today, the study is viewed with skepticism. Zimbardo, by playing the prison superintendent, was no objective observer, and the study lacked clear criteria of what was being measured. The authors of a recent replication televised by the BBC contest Zimbardo's claims that social roles and uniforms are enough to transform people. In their study the guards splintered, uncomfortable about their mandate and power. The prisoners organized and negotiated new terms. The mind can be a jailer, but only if you choose it.

ORDINARY PEOPLE, SIMPLY DOING THEIR JOBS, AND WITHOUT ANY PARTICULAR HOSTILITY ON THEIR PART, CAN BECOME AGENTS IN A TERRIBLE DESTRUCTIVE PROCESS.

43

STANLEY MILGRAM
1933-1984

SOURCE: *Obedience to Authority*
DATE: 1974
FIELD: Social psychology

Haunted by impact of the Holocaust on his family, Stanley Milgram became preoccupied with the power of authority to incite evil acts. His obedience experiments were his attempt to understand it. Participants were told their job was to use electric shocks when mistakes were made by a test-taking subject restrained in an adjacent room. A white-coated experimenter urged the participant to give increasingly stronger shocks—well beyond the shock level marked "safe"—disregarding audible pleas from the subject for release.

Two-thirds of participants gave the maximum shock, surprising students and peers, who had predicted this would be extremely rare. (Thankfully, the subjects and shocks were fake.) It didn't surprise Milgram, who anticipated that the authority of the scientist would lead participants to put aside personal responsibility: They were just a cog in the machine, just following orders. To Milgram, this seemed to explain participation in Nazi atrocities, especially the bureaucrats involved in the Holocaust. After the Vietnam War's My Lai atrocity, Milgram suggested that preventing such massacres would involve reviewing the obedience to authority integral to US military training.

Milgram's work has since been reevaluated, in its ethics, its methods (the scientist could be so relentless it questions whether participants were obeying instructions or submitting to coercion), and the validity of results, as it appears likely many participants saw through the entire ruse. Yet replications confirm authority has a strong influence on behavior, and evidence suggests your brain responds differently to freely chosen actions as it does to instructed ones. We can resist, but compliance has a powerful pull.

Without consciousness the mind–body problem would be much less interesting. With consciousness it seems hopeless.

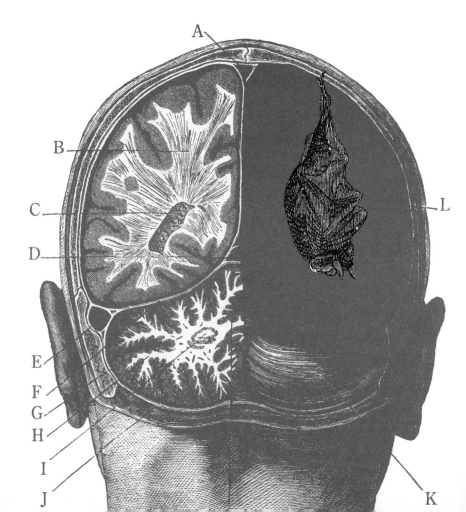

44

THOMAS NAGEL
b. 1937

SOURCE: "What Is It Like to Be a Bat?"
DATE: 1974
FIELD: Existentialist

How do our minds relate to our bodies? Are they separate, as René Descartes proposed, or indelibly intertwined? A third view that became popular in the 20th century proposes that the mind is simply the product of the body, specifically the brain. In its extreme form of "eliminative reductionism," there is no mind to speak of—we're simply confused because we haven't yet figured out the biology. However, philosopher of mind Thomas Nagel saw an elephant in the room: consciousness. We have a sense of ourselves—not merely a practical account, like an operating system that can catalog its own files, but a subjective, unique feeling of being *this* me, now.

Nagel illustrated the point with a bat. We can undoubtedly list aspects of "batness": A bat flies, hangs upside-down, navigates by a special sense. Yet we have absolutely no way into the bat's sense of being itself, which remains impossibly foreign. Nagel was illustrating the "qualia" of batness—the unique subjective experience of that state. Isaac Newton struggled with this idea centuries earlier when wondering how light "produceth in our minds the phantasm of color."

Nagel argued that without an account of how objective material could create subjective experience, we can't assume that "brain explains mind." The philosopher David Chalmers later called this the hard problem of consciousness, because practical scientific advances (eg, understanding how we focus our awareness) don't seem likely to clarify this issue. The debate rages on, and philosophers of mind take positions anywhere from reductionism to panpsychism, the idea that consciousness is found in everything.

HE WAS DEAD.
DESTROYED BY ORDER
OF THE COURT,
ENFORCED BY THE
TRANSMISSION OF
HIGH-VOLTAGE
ALTERNATING CURRENT
THROUGH THE LOBES
OF HIS BRAIN.

45

ROBERT PIRSIG
1928–2017

SOURCE: *Zen and the Art of Motorcycle Maintenance*
DATE: 1974
FIELD: Psychiatry

Robert Pirsig was a restless, brilliant mind seeking to understand the very nature of reality. His semiautobiographical masterwork, *Zen and the Art of Motorcycle Maintenance*, discusses these issues through the story of a genius friend, Phaedrus, whose quest for the truth had killed him. Late in the book, Pirsig as narrator reveals that Phaedrus was no friend, but himself—institutionalized and put through what was then called electroshock therapy. Post-"cure," a version of him survived, but his memories of that time, and the Phaedrus he had been, were now dead. It is a brutal portrayal of what we now call electroconvulsive therapy, or ECT.

ECT was certainly overused in the past, frequently without the patient consent now required outside of the most exceptional circumstances. It is typically a course of last resort for treatment-resistant conditions such as severe depression, catatonia, or long-lasting psychotic episodes, and always administered under anesthetic to minimize discomfort. A large majority of patients who receive ECT report improvement. We don't know exactly why. We can track the associated brain changes, but poorly understand how these banish depression and other symptoms. ECT remains controversial, with some individuals and clinicians insisting that it is harmful.

Though not, it seems, for Pirsig—at least, not as we were told. Unearthed documents reveal his account of ECT as personality death was a literary device used to shape his story: It was the fictional Pirsig suffering from gaps in his past, not Pirsig the author. When it comes to this most arcane of mental treatments, it's hard to unpick the truth from fiction.

It is better to have enough ideas for some of them to be wrong, than to be always right by having no ideas at all

EDWARD DE BONO
b. 1933

SOURCE: *Lateral Thinking: A Textbook of Creativity*
DATE: 1977
FIELD: Creativity and potential

Edward Charles Francis Publius de Bono. That name, and de Bono's early accomplishments—medic, Rhodes scholar, breaker of canoeing records—bring to mind an aristocratic figure in a private dining room, waving a cigar nostalgically over the crumbs of an expensive meal. Yet de Bono is no traditionalist; he's an evangelist for new ways of thinking, above all, creative thinking. He believes that society trains us to be mentally vertical—narrow and focused—when we should be lateral, exploring different or surprising options. For de Bono, criticism and analysis is only one mode of thinking. In his "thinking hats" metaphor, he encouraged people to deliberately switch between modes at different stages—the blue hat for big picture, the white hat for the facts, the green hat for creative investigations, and sparing use of the black hat for critical evaluation (we must be free to explore before we are judged).

De Bono encouraged others to entertain wild ideas, and he practiced what he preached. Would anyone else have suggested we could solve the Arab-Israeli conflict by shipping in jars of the British zinc-rich sandwich spread Marmite? (He believed that the low levels of zinc in unleavened bread could contribute to aggression.) He even developed a number-based code to replace human language. Creativity researchers see de Bono as an enthusiast rather than a serious scholar, and it's true that his many techniques are rarely validated scientifically. His popularizations have, however, managed to capture many truths about creativity: You can't do it without being willing to explore, take risks, and fail along the way.

Clean

A   Just out of the bathtub

B   Very well dressed

C   Very religious

D   Has a great deal

ROBERT WILLIAMS
b. 1930

SOURCE: Black Intelligence Test of Cultural Homogeneity
DATE: 1972
FIELD: Psychometrics

There was some consternation in the field of psychology tests when Robert
Williams announced his new creation. In truth, the Black Intelligence Test of
Cultural Homogeneity—shortened to BITCH—was designed to ruffle feathers.
As a black psychologist, Williams was dismayed that IQ tests, on which black
people tended to score poorly, were frequently laced with assumptions from
white culture. In the workforce, he held his own intellectually compared with
his white peers, but was frustrated that his earlier test scores had suggested he
possessed only a mediocre mind.

So Williams made his own test, structured in a familiar way, with definitional
questions laid out in multiple choice format. Yet the questions referred
specifically to things familiar to black people, from their vernacular and
environment, such as the alley apple (a brick), black draught (a folk remedy
and laxative), and a crib (home). When it was administered to high-school
students in St. Louis, he found the black ones scored comparatively much
better—87 percent accuracy, versus just 51 percent in white students. He had
made his point.

Before Williams, psychologists had recognized that cultural factors could bias
tests, with an early attempt at addressing this made by Raymond Cattell in
1949. Yet a truly acultural test is deceptively difficult, some say impossible.
Familiarity with taking a test itself affects performance and varies culturally.
Since Williams' work, decades of tracking the black–white testing gap suggests it
is shrinking, supporting his hunch that testing and cultural factors, rather than
fundamental differences, are at its heart.

Any natural, normal human being, when faced with any kind of loss, will go from shock all the way through acceptance.

48

ELISABETH KÜBLER-ROSS
1926–2004

SOURCE: Interview in *Playboy* magazine
DATE: 1981
FIELD: Well-being

In 1969 the Swiss-American psychiatrist Elisabeth Kübler-Ross published *On Death and Dying*, a case for improving the end-of-life experience. Her work with the terminally ill had revealed many issues. For instance, doctors still deliberated whether to tell patients they were going to die—a question Kübler-Ross considered both patronizing and a sign that physicians hadn't come to terms with mortality. She believed everyone should be given the chance to use their remaining time well and meet death with open eyes.

Kübler-Ross believed patients facing their own death went through a series of "stages of grief"—denial, anger, bargaining, depression, and acceptance—each a bridge to the next. She developed these stages through intuition rather than systematic analysis. Furthermore, over time she allowed it to be applied more and more broadly, even to ending relationships or job redundancies. Unsurprisingly, the model has shortcomings. Acceptance seems to come much earlier than suggested, and anger, although common, may not be necessary, and encouraging it may simply prolong distress.

In later life, Kübler-Ross became interested in near-death experiences and life after death. "I didn't believe in ghosts. But I've had some experiences, personally, that have just blown my mind." This journey sadly took her into credulous contact with unsavory charlatans, and these errors of judgment tarnished her legacy. Nevertheless, she gave a voice to the nature of grief in all its contradictions. Her model penetrated the public consciousness and has been exploited as a narrative structure by movies such as *Blade Runner* and *Groundhog Day*.

A pattern of emotional overload and subsequent emotional exhaustion is at the heart of the burnout syndrome.

49

CHRISTINA MASLACH
b. 1946

SOURCE: *Burnout: The Cost of Caring*
DATE: 1982
FIELD: Well-being

Early in her research career, Christina Maslach saw firsthand the emotional damage done by dysfunctional environments. She was a junior member of the team running the notorious Stanford Prison Experiment (see page 89). Maslach saw how the volunteers were being harmed by the situation, and was the one to demand the experiment be ended early. In her subsequent research on work-related stress, she was skeptical about explanations that focused on the individual—that stress resulted from personal sickness, weak character, or a bullying bad apple. "Imagine investigating the personality of cucumbers to discover why they had turned into sour pickles without analyzing the vinegar barrels in which they had been submerged," she wrote. Instead, consider the system.

Maslach interviewed police officers, nurses, and teachers experiencing what she would call burnout. The same themes came up repeatedly: long hours, unjust environments, lack of impact of their work. In particular were impossible emotional demands, like staying calm in the face of tantrums or traumas. At the end of the day they would change out of their work clothes but found it harder to shed the psychological armor they wore to cope with these challenges. Despite initial resistance from the academic community, burnout turned out to resonate with huge numbers of people, and the concept is taken seriously by workplaces worldwide. The cure to burnout is not inactivity; people seek out work to give structure and satisfaction. What's crucial is balance, as Maslach emphasizes: "Balance between giving and getting, balance between stress and calm, balance between work and home."

Everything can be taken from a man but one thing: the last of human freedoms—to choose one's attitude in any given set of circumstances, to **choose one's own way.**

50

VIKTOR FRANKL
1905–1997

SOURCE: *Man's Search for Meaning*
DATE: 1985
FIELD: Existentialism

What meaning can you take away from the Nazi death camps? This question was drawn from the personal experiences of Austrian neurologist and psychiatrist Viktor Frankl. He had been building an impressive career, working with the pioneering clinicians Sigmund Freud (see page 29) and Alfred Adler (see page 69), and creating a school counseling service in Vienna. However, this was disrupted when the Nazis took over his country. For a time he continued his work, using his hospital position to save patients from euthanasia. Even once forced into the ghetto, he set up a mental health service and suicide watch for inhabitants.

Finally came the camps: Auschwitz, Kaufering, Türkheim. Frankl survived, but his mother, brother, and wife did not. Afterward these experiences informed his existential approach to psychological healing, logotherapy, which he promoted through books and lectures. It centered on existential questions about death, freedom, and the meaning of life. Even in the most painful and degrading situation, he insisted, life contains meaning. By the same token, one can be existentially sick while living in comfort, if meaning has been lost. Ultimately, meaning is more powerful than suffering.

What that means for us is a balance between freedom and responsibility—without the latter, there can be no meaning, only arbitrariness. *Man's Search for Meaning* is the title of Frankl's book, and it sums up well his mission—as do the book's earlier titles, *From Death-Camp to Existentialism* and *Nevertheless, Say "Yes" to Life* (a translation of the title of the original German-language edition of the book).

He reached out his hand, and
took hold of his wife's head,
tried to lift it, to put it on.
He had apparently mistaken
his wife for a hat!

51

OLIVER SACKS
1933-2015

SOURCE: *The Man Who Mistook His Wife for a Hat and Other Clinical Tales*
DATE: 1985
FIELD: Neuropsychology

British-born Oliver Sacks was a neurologist and writer who, during a career in American hospitals, documented curious cases that showed the public an undiscovered world. Neurological damage can transform our experience in profound ways, and Sacks wrote about this thoughtfully and compassionately, often showing that neurological deficits could be accompanied by unexpected gains. He described a group of patients laughing derisively at a presidential speech on TV. They all had aphasia—a deficit in understanding language—but through reading tone and body language quickly saw through the "sincerity" of the performance.

Sacks was initially skeptical about whether the visual complaint of his new patient "Dr. P" was really neurological—he seemed so charming and coherent, though not for long. When Dr. P was asked to replace his shoe after a foot examination, he became uncertain which was the shoe and which the foot. He could pick out details in a landscape picture but could not grasp what the whole depicted. At the end of the appointment came the quoted moment. Dr. P's difficulties, due to atypical progression of Alzheimer's disease, were a striking example of visual agnosia—the inability to recognize what the eyes see. (Much later in life, Sacks came to recognize that his difficulty recognizing others, that had exacerbated his lifelong shyness, was itself due to an agnosia.)

This story has been immortalized in Michael Nyman's opera named for Sacks' book, and the Robert de Niro movie *Awakenings* is based on Sacks' account of sleeping sickness. His influence on art, together with his own writing, led the *New York Times* to dub Sacks a "poet laureate of contemporary medicine."

The propensity to make strong emotional bonds to particular individuals is a basic component of human nature.

52

JOHN BOWLBY
1907–1990

SOURCE: *A Secure Base*
DATE: 1988
FIELD: Child development

John Bowlby lived an isolated childhood. His well-to-do parents took the view that affection would spoil him, so he was raised by servants and at boarding school. This isolated beginning may have suited him for working with troubled children, as he did as a teacher and after psychiatric and psychoanalytical training, including with wartime evacuees. He assembled these experiences in his first book, *44 Thieves*, where he noted that many of his delinquent cases had experienced prolonged separation from caregivers in their early life.

He became convinced this separation was significant. Inspired by the work animal ethologists were doing on mothers and young, he theorized that babies develop an attachment to adults who interact with them. Moreover, this link teaches them both how to be and how to expect others to treat them. Bowlby developed this attachment theory with Mary Ainsworth, creator of the "strange situation" procedure. Here, experimenters observe a baby's reactions as their mother alternately plays with it and leaves it in the company of a stranger. The reactions betray different styles of attachment, such as anxious-avoidant, where the child reacts to events in a cool, even passive manner, while agitated beneath the surface (shown by increased heart rate), or the anxious-resistant child, who quickly becomes distressed.

Ideally, the child is securely attached. These styles persevere into adulthood, but we are still figuring out whether a style develops due to the parent's actions or is inherited genetically. Recent work suggests that we can exhibit different styles with different people, which complicates the original theory. Despite these nuances, attachment's place in psychology is secure.

WE PERCEIVE REALITY THROUGH A VEIL OF UNCONSCIOUS FANTASY.

53

JANET MALCOLM
b. 1934

SOURCE: *Psychoanalysis: The Impossible Profession*
DATE: 1988
FIELD: Perceptions and biases

Janet Malcolm is a pugnacious writer who was born in Czechoslovakia and raised in America. She is well versed in psychoanalysis, and her writing displays its appetite for speculating on motivations, which got her (unsuccessfully) sued for libel after writing an eviscerating critique of a prominent US analyst. Here Malcolm describes fantasy, a preoccupation in many strains of analytical thought. Melanie Klein, a key post-Freudian figure, argued that relationships are mediated by our visions of past ones. We do not relate to our boss, but to a projection of our father. Meanwhile, Carl Jung (see page 55) suggested that we pour fantasy into our romantic relationships; instead of the object of our affection, we see our notion of the ideal woman or man.

There is a growing consensus in psychology that, indeed, we do not see what there is. Most of our visual experience is not a faithful reading of the outside world, but is filled in by our brain, according to its best guesses. We relate to the world functionally, according to our needs—food, resting place, threat— so we cannot see what doesn't matter (see page 179). This is a very old idea that can be found in the Hindu concept of *maya*, Plato's allegory of the cave, and even preclassical warnings of the power of Aphrodite to cloud us in desire. Throughout history, meditation practitioners have claimed it is possible to pass through the veil and see things as they actually are. Whether these claims can be verified by psychological exploration, or only by personal experience, is yet to be determined.

ENJOYMENT APPEARS AT THE BOUNDARY BETWEEN BOREDOM AND ANXIETY, WHEN THE CHALLENGES ARE JUST BALANCED WITH THE PERSON'S CAPACITY TO A

54

MIHÁLY CSÍKSZENTMIHÁLYI
b. 1934

SOURCE: *The Psychology of Optimal Experience*
DATE: 1990
FIELD: Creativity and potential

Mihály Csíkszentmihályi is the grandmaster of flow. In this psychological state, everything beyond the activity melts away, and you do what you are doing simply because you are doing it. Csíkszentmihályi noticed this phenomenon in artists who would forget to eat or sleep when deep in their work. His investigations show that flow requires the right kinds of activity, a level of challenge that just pushes at your capacity to meet it. This can be interpreted somewhat mystically, such as the psychologist Jordan Peterson's take: It's a signal from reality to stick with whatever problem you are tackling, because you seem to be the right person to solve it. Csíkszentmihályi himself notes the resemblance flow has to the Taoist concept of *wu wei*. Best described as doing without doing, this is when your actions are in harmony with the natural way of being, and so do not require further effort to do.

During flow your sense of passing time warps and you lose self-consciousness. This will be familiar to committed martial artists, who might know it as *budō* or *muchin*. Flow is also a huge deal in competition and sports psychology, through notions such as "the inner game" and "getting in the zone." Sports competitors who break records or attain other peak performance frequently describe out-of-body experiences or the sense of not having to try. Group flow is also possible—drummers and bassists call it being "in the pocket," and comedic improvisers emphasize "group mind," whereby ideas seem to arrive to everyone together. Csíkszentmihályi considers flow experiences as optimal experiences, key to healthy and meaningful lives, and the concept is a cornerstone of the positive psychology movement aimed at helping us to live such lives.

Given appropriate
social conditions,
decent, ordinary
people can be led to
do extraordinarily
cruel things.

55

ALBERT BANDURA
b. 1925

SOURCE: *Origins of Terrorism: Psychologies, Ideologies, Theologies, States of Mind*
DATE: 1990
FIELD: Child development

Often described as the greatest living psychologist, Albert Bandura is known for many contributions to the field, but foremost is his understanding of human cruelty and aggression. During the 1960s the Canadian-American showed how aggression is learned not just through being rewarded or punished, as behaviorism had demonstrated, but by modeling behavior seen around us. His classic Bobo doll experiment showed that nursery-aged children who observe an adult repeatedly striking a doll and yelling are more likely to reproduce this behavior. However, should they witness the adult reprimanded for their behavior, their appetite wanes, showing sensitivity to the wider social world. Similar effects occurred with a live clown in place of a doll, and even when a cartoon cat was the perpetrator—thus Bandura became one of the first psychologists to explore the effect of violence in the media.

Bandura had shown a way by which role models shape our appetite for violence. Yet he wasn't content to leave it there—after all, a boy raised around domestic abuse may pledge to never allow it to happen. Bandura became interested in our ethical standards, and what led us to put these standards aside. The answer was moral justification: People would commit terrible acts that were framed as necessary for the nation, faith, or the "bigger picture"; people would tolerate them when cloaked in euphemisms like "collateral damage." So Bandura documented two features of human malevolence: the power of role modeling to present cruelty as an option, and the power of moral justification to present it as a duty.

9:06

Now I am ~~Perfectly, Overwhelmingly~~ awake

9:34

Now I am ~~superlatively, actually~~ awake

9:40

Now I am ~~magnificently, perfectly~~ awake.

56

CLIVE WEARING
b. 1938

SOURCE: Diary entry
DATE: 1990
FIELD: Memory

Clive Wearing was once an accomplished musician, a respected choral singer at Westminster Cathedral with a mastery of the piano. His life was irrevocably changed, however, by the brain disease herpesviral encephalitis. It took his ability to store new memories, meaning that new experiences would dissipate after just seconds. The crossings-out in his diary reflect what this feels like to him.

Wearing's situation echoes one of the most important cases of memory dysfunction, relating to the subject "HM," whose problems began after a lobectomy to treat his epilepsy. Over decades his deficits were explored by neuropsychologists led by the pioneering Brenda Milner, using his condition to explore the relationship between different brain functions. HM could not forge new memories, but could access ones from early in his life, helping confirm that these aspects of memory, new encoding and past retrieval, are separate. However, HM could not access memories from shortly before his surgery. This suggested that freshly made memories are stored in one part of the brain (the temporal lobe areas lost by HM) but over time are moved from this hub to be distributed across the brain.

Similarly, Wearing's condition reminds us of the multifaceted nature of memory. Despite more widespread amnesia than even HM, he still remembers and feels deep love for his second wife, who he married shortly before the illness, and, although Wearing has lost a great deal, he hasn't lost the music.

"I SMELL BURNT TOAST!"

57

DRAMATIZATION, UNNAMED PATIENT OF WILDER PENFIELD
1891–1976

SOURCE: Canadian Public Service Announcement
DATE: Published 1991 (originally 1934)
FIELD: Neuropsychology

Wilder Penfield was born in the USA and moved to Canada, becoming the country's first neurosurgeon and later being honored as a National Historic Person, in recognition of his pioneering medical work. Penfield's accomplishments are extensive: developing brain-cell staining techniques, implementing less damaging surgical approaches, and founding the first (of many) hospitals incorporating a brain research unit.

The quoted event is well known to Canadians of a certain age as the topic of a short documentary featured between commercials. Penfield had a patient whose seizures were augured by the smell of burnt toast. He had developed a technique that could use such clues to find the neural cells causing the seizure. With the top of their skull removed, conscious patients could give him feedback as to the effects of electrodes applied to brain areas. In this case, Penfield was able to elicit the toast smell, surgically remove the area, and eliminate the seizure.

As well as altering lives, this technique altered our understanding of the brain. His investigations uncovered brain body maps (see page 179), and identified a range of phenomena tied to the temporal lobes of the brain. His electrical probe could generate recall of memories, emotions such as loneliness and fear, déjà vu (see page 75), and even dreams, hallucinations, and out-of-body experiences. Penfield also employed his skills toward personal needs: He performed complex surgery on his sister, delaying for years her death from brain cancer. There's no doubt that Canada's award was a well-judged one.

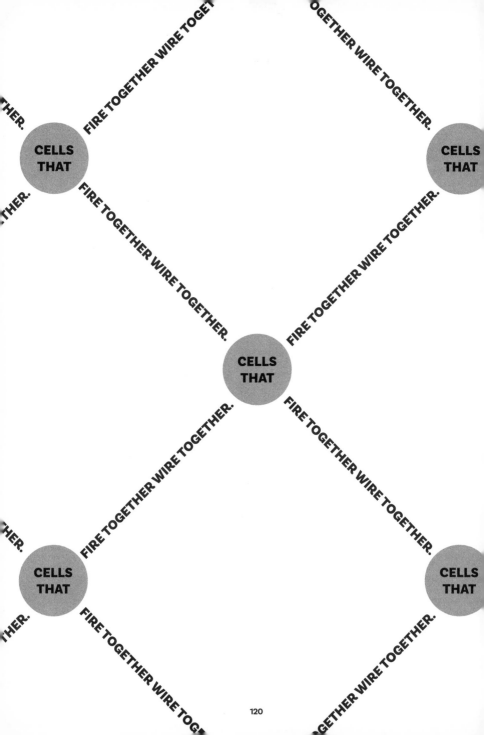

58

CARLA SHATZ
b. 1947

SOURCE: The article "The Developing Brain"
DATE: 1992
FIELD: Neuropsychology

The first usage in print of the quote opposite was by neuroscientist Siegrid Löwel, but it's widely understood that Carla Shatz had already coined the phrase over years of lectures on the biology of the maturing brain. It pithily summarizes an insight by Donald Hebb, whose work was critical in connecting brain and mind together. Hebbian learning is the process by which neurons strengthen connections through use. Technically, one fires *just* before the other, so the second can incorporate the earlier event into its own habits, but "fire together, wire together" captures the core idea succinctly.

We can get a close look at this through Shatz's own work. In theory, the brain could develop in the same way a house is developed from initial blueprints, systematically following steps encoded in strict instructions (in the case of the brain, DNA), from foundations to the final lick of paint. It doesn't work that way, however. Instead, the brain quickly grows sufficient neurons to be raw material. Then the brain actively tries to find its way to a finished state, through a process involving trial and error. For instance, neurons generated in the eye are looking for destinations in the visual areas of the brain, but they lack a precise map. The neurons use sensors at their tips to help them feel out the next viable step in their pathway "home." When mistakes are made, the fire-and-wire reinforcement ensures that routes that are better at carrying visual information all the way from start to finish get strengthened, while other ones are eliminated. Even before we are born, our brains have been on a journey to become what they are.

"HEY BUDDY, CAN YOU SPARE

CENTS?"

59

UNKNOWN RESEARCH ASSISTANT, ADVISED BY MICHAEL D. SANTOS, CRAIG LEVE AND ANTHONY R. PRATKANIS

SOURCE: The article "'Hey Buddy, Can You Spare Seventeen Cents?' Mindful Persuasion and the Pique Technique"
DATE: 1994
FIELD: Social psychology

To study the specifics of persuasion, a trio of University of California researchers set up an unorthodox study. Experimenters posing as panhandlers hung out on Santa Cruz wharf and asked passers-by the pointed question quoted opposite. It generated more conversation and take-home cash than the generic, "Can you spare a dime?", showing that specificity works. By piquing curiosity, it shook people out of their automatic scripts; this wasn't just ambient urban noise, it was a real person with a specific need of some kind.

Specificity is one of many persuasion factors uncovered by psychologists. The best overview is Robert Cialdini's, who has amassed six principles of persuasion. Some of these are described elsewhere—authority (see page 91) and consensus (see page 67). Another is scarcity: People are keener to acquire something that seems rare ("While stocks last!"). The principle of reciprocity is also important: If you scratch someone's back, they are more likely to scratch yours, which explains the chocolate your waiter gives you just before you decide on his tip. Then there's consistency. People dislike contradicting themselves, so if they can be led to show any kind of appreciation for a product, there is more chance they will end up walking away with it. Also, we are happier to agree with those whom we like.

People with training in psychology can be found in the sales and marketing divisions of numerous companies. Nowadays, charities, health organizations, and public policy units also engage in persuasion. Everyone wants to influence, from politicians in the halls of government to the person with a tin mug on the street corner.

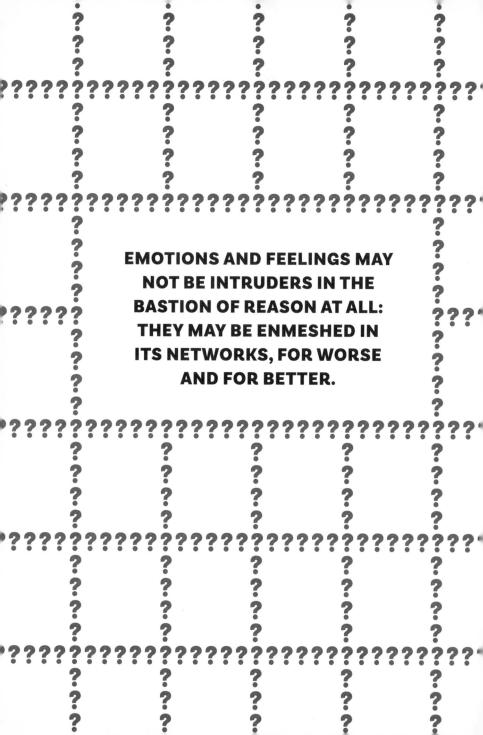

EMOTIONS AND FEELINGS MAY
NOT BE INTRUDERS IN THE
BASTION OF REASON AT ALL:
THEY MAY BE ENMESHED IN
ITS NETWORKS, FOR WORSE
AND FOR BETTER.

60

ANTONIO DAMASIO
b. 1944

SOURCE: *Descartes' Error*
DATE: 1994
FIELD: Emotion

It can be tempting to want humans to be more like *Star Trek*'s Vulcans, making decisions without distraction from pesky emotions. Yet the work of Portuguese-American neuroscientist Antonio Damasio suggests this wouldn't turn out like the movies. His work with patients with brain damage led him to suspect that decision-making and emotional abilities were intertwined. He investigated this in experiments where people gambled in a computerized game, picking cards from different onscreen decks. All decks had better and worse-scoring cards, but some were on average "good" and others "bad."

Patients with deficits in emotion would struggle to score well, while the healthy participants homed in on the good decks. They were assisted in this by reactions made by their bodies—when they hovered the computer cursor near a bad deck, sweat monitors showed their stress response jumped up, even before they had become consciously aware there was anything bad about it. The body had generated an emotional record of the past losses—a "somatic marker," in Damasio's words—that guided decision-making, even before the mind could make sense of it.

Damasio believed that every day we make countless decisions in this way, feelings communicated through our bodies guiding us to the more relaxing, attractive, or reassuring option, without having to call for conscious analysis from the mind. Damasio credits his views as being foreshadowed by the ideas of philosopher Baruch Spinoza, who challenged the notion that mind was separate from body, and argued instead that we deeply depend on bodily sensation to think.

LANGUAGE IS AN INSTINCT

LANGUAGE IS NOT AN INSTINCT

61

STEVEN PINKER / MICHAEL TOMASELLO
b. 1954 / b. 1950

SOURCE: *The Language Instinct* / The book review "Language is not an instinct"
DATE: 1994 / 1995
FIELD: Language

Steven Pinker and Michael Tomasello are both authorities in the fields of linguistics and psychology. Their opposing quotes summarize a long-running argument: whether our capacity for language is narrowly evolved and bounded. Pinker argues that, yes, there is a universal grammar (UG) designed into the brain, a general framework just waiting to know if it should operate by the specific rules of Mandarin or Yoruba. Evidence from this comes from Noam Chomsky's original case for linguistic complexity (see page 73), as well as vivid examples, such as how displaced people who speak a common crude pidgin have children who fill in the missing grammar to create a nuanced creole.

Yet the argument is far from settled. In reviewing Pinker's book, Tomasello pointed out that instincts are predictable and develop even in total isolation; language does not. He agreed that in some sense our brains are language-ready—they have a learning ability and short-term memory that allows for sequencing remembered items (whether syllables or notes on piano keys). Yet he argues that language grows from these general features, together with other psychological abilities like symbolic thinking, imagery, and mental schemes, rather than a discrete, abstracted grammar module.

Lately, the case for UG has been rocked by the documentation of fundamentally different grammars that don't fit with the model: some lacking adjectives, others reportedly both verbs and nouns; some working through sentences, some through ever-longer compound words. Neuroscience seems to suggest that there is no circumscribed module in the brain—language involves activity everywhere. Instinctual, or emergent? The jury is still out.

Do parents have any long-term effects on the development of their child's personality?

NO.

THE ANSWER IS

62

JUDITH RICH HARRIS
b. 1938

SOURCE: *The Nurture Assumption: Why Children Turn Out the Way They Do*
DATE: 1995
FIELD: Child development

In her landmark journal paper, Judith Rich Harris has a modest affiliation: Middletown, New Jersey. She hadn't attended an academic institute, and she had no PhD; she was a textbook editor whose sharp mind had seen a problem. Psychologists and the public took for granted that parenting had a huge impact on children, justifying an industry of manuals, courses, and help columns. However, Harris was well-read in the burgeoning field of behavioral genetics and knew its major tools: studies tracking differences between identical and nonidentical twins, and adoption studies tracking similarities between genetic siblings raised in different households.

She mainstreamed their findings through a paper and then a book, *The Nurture Assumption*. It argued that parents influence their children through their DNA, not their parenting decisions. The "shared environment" of the family had little to no effect on traits like intelligence, personality, or motivation. There was a nongenetic contribution, but not from the household; Harris argued it was peer socialization, what you pick up from your friends. Don't worry about your parenting style, she stressed—it doesn't matter much.

Harris' work was praised effusively by some—Steven Pinker (see page 127) cites her extensively in his book *The Blank Slate*. Others were hostile. The consensus nowadays is that Harris' rhetorical reframing is excessive. The shared environment does matter, and moreover the genetics approach ignores nonshared factors in a family, like a parent proud of one child, disappointed in another. Yet the genetic genie has sprung the bottle, and any discussion of parental effects must contend with it.

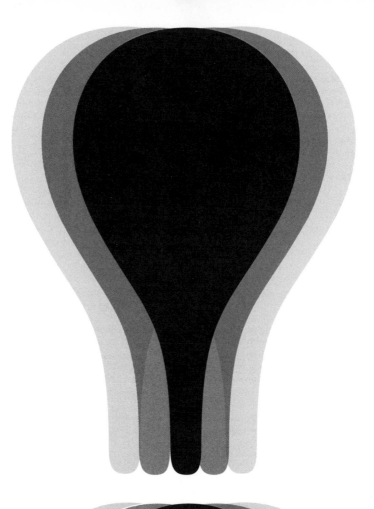

Intelligence
is what you
use when you
don't know
what to do.

WILLIAM H. CALVIN
b. 1939

SOURCE: *How Brains Think*
DATE: 1996
FIELD: Psychometrics

What is intelligence? We might look for it in the accumulation of facts or the perfection of skills, but it actually lies elsewhere. Jean Piaget (see page 45) captures it best, nicely paraphrased here by neurophysiologist William H. Calvin. Intelligence is the inquiring impulse found in us and animals alike that allows for improvisation, exploration, and new approaches to dealing with the world. Piaget's insights came from working with children, who frequently butted up against the unknown, the new, and the contradictory. They would then explore, and pay attention.

Intelligence is how humans discover patterns, internalize them, and then use them to more effectively navigate their reality. Calvin's interest is in how this evolved: Why are we flexible generalists rather than exquisitely specialized for a narrow environmental niche? He suggests that periods of climate change meant that the environment kept shifting for our ancestors, so it was necessary to be ready for anything.

Over the years, attempts to measure intelligence have been justly criticized. Yet thanks partly to this scrutiny, intelligence has become the most robust construct ever developed in the discipline. While individuals may have particular strengths, such as being more mathematical than verbal, it seems clear that these are underpinned by a more general intelligence factor, which the British psychologist Charles Spearman termed the "g" factor. G is supported by our working memory capacity—how many things we can hold in mind at once—and the speed at which we process information. It's the horsepower of the intelligence engine, powering us through the unknown.

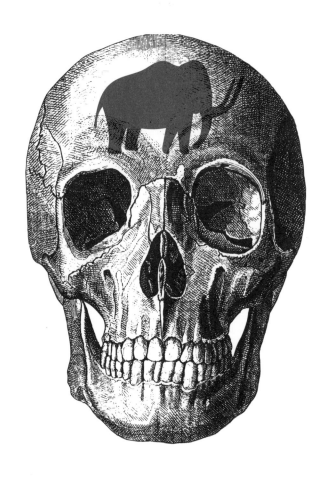

Our **modern** skulls
house a Stone Age **mind**.

64

LEDA COSMIDES
b. 1957

SOURCE: *Evolutionary Psychology: A Primer*
DATE: 1997
FIELD: Human universals

The psychologist Leda Cosmides began her studies as a biologist. This provided her with a powerful lens—evolutionary theory—that had been underused in psychology. With Jerome Barkow and stalwart collaborator (and husband) John Tooby, she edited *The Adapted Mind*, a broadside against three assumptions they believed dominated the social sciences. That firstly, all facets of human existence are socially constructed; secondly, culture shapes everything; and finally, the mind is receptive to whatever comes—a perfectly blank slate.

Cosmides and Tooby have been the principal advocates for another perspective, that the mind is built according to a set of evolutionary constraints. It exists to solve a number of specific problems, with different hardwired mental "organs" or modules evolved for each one, akin to a Swiss army knife. These problems must have been present over long stretches of evolutionary time, mostly during our past as savanna hunter-gatherers, and led to the development of universal features of human psychology. They include things like reading sexual cues, spotting untrustworthiness, and detecting predators. If the mind was no blank slate, then it could push back against culture and shape it in return, reproducing features of our evolutionary past in the present.

Other psychologists contest this. Our brains may not be blank, but they are very flexible, and develop with less fidelity to deep-rooted design than we had imagined (see page 121). Explanations based on speculation about unseen ancestors have been critiqued as "just-so stories," but most psychologists agree that our minds are not endlessly malleable. When we long for trees and sunlight or a slower pace of life, we may be expressing our evolved preferences.

Why are all the black kids sitting together in the cafeteria?

65

BEVERLY DANIEL TATUM
b. 1954

SOURCE: *Why Are All the Black Kids Sitting Together in the Cafeteria?*
DATE: 1997
FIELD: Identity

Having been born just after racial segregation was abolished, Floridian Beverly Daniel Tatum got to attend school in an overwhelmingly white milieu. She noticed that during elementary school, kids would mix with little regard for race. However, in high school that gave way to what seemed like a self-imposed segregation. Her book attempts to answer why. Tatum observes that as young people from minorities get older, they pass into new social categories, like from "cute black boy" to "tall black youth." Now, older ladies give them a wide berth on the street, and suspicious detectives follow them around stores. Their white friends have no reference point for these troubling experiences, so they are drawn to spend more time with people who have. That's why the black kids sit together in the cafeteria.

Tatum is now an advocate for arresting this drift. She recommends leaving kids free to choose their own company during free time, but using class to encourage different configurations to work together. Schools could encourage participation in rewarding but white-dominated activities like student committees. Sensitive issues like slavery can be tackled smartly. Rather than crafting narratives about victims and oppressors that make both black and white kids retreat uneasily, you can focus your narratives on white abolitionists and empowered black individuals like Harriet Tubman, so that students can focus on common ground rather than division. Come 2017, when Tatum rereleased her book, racial identity had taken a new centrality in politics. Reflecting on the challenges she saw ahead, she wrote, "With the collective hard work and effort of many, I still believe positive social change is possible."

It's not just top-down culture that socializes us into genders. The genders of those we interact with brings out our notions of gender.

66

ELEANOR MACCOBY
b. 1917

SOURCE: *The Two Sexes: Growing Up Apart, Coming Together*
DATE: 1998
FIELD: Identity

Eleanor Maccoby, now a centenarian, was born into a society with fixed ideas about gender. She set about interrogating these ideas from a fiercely independent vantage point, developed perhaps through her unconventional upbringing by vegetarian parents interested in Eastern thought. Her book *The Psychology of Sex Differences* showed that many such differences were mere prejudice, such as claims that girls were more suggestible or less motivated than boys. To write it she combed through both published and unpublished research, realizing that for every published claim of sex difference, there were often many failed attempts at replication. This was an early attempt to combat the "file drawer effect," whereby studies with insignificant effects are never published and quietly filed away, which we now know can severely distort a field of research.

Later Maccoby realized that trying to characterize a girl or boy in the abstract might be the wrong approach entirely. Her work showed that a young child of either sex left alone in a playroom behaves very similarly. Two boys together would move and play, whereas two girls would be more likely to sit and talk. The presence of gendered cues helped gender emerge: Boys create a safe space for "boyness," just as girls do for "girlness." Years of investigating these interactions across time and cultures led her to a nuanced view: Socialization is important, but the differences that are responded to socially originated in biological differences. She suspected that this view put a rift between her and her contemporaries in the feminist movement, but her iconoclasm was true to form, and her conclusions, as ever, based on the data.

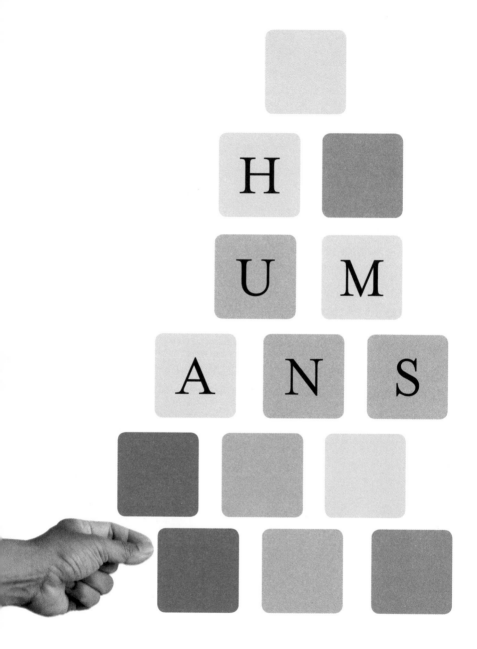

ARE A UNIQUELY PLAYFUL SPECIES.

67

JAAK PANKSEPP
1943-2017

SOURCE: *Affective Neuroscience: The Foundations of Human and Animal Emotions*
DATE: 1998
FIELD: Creativity and potential

Estonia-born Jaak Panksepp expected his interests in emotion would make clinical psychology an ideal career. However, he discovered therapy at that time was focused on modifying external behavior, and made a surprising turn—into veterinary departments to study rats. This switch led him to found the field of affective neuroscience, the investigation of emotion in the brain.

Panksepp identified a number of "primary processes"—emotion-circuits deep in rats' brains. Among powerful emotions like fear, rage, and lust, you might be surprised that one of these fundamentals is play. Yet it turns out there is a mammalian play brain circuit, dedicated to social exploration, mock combat, and surprise. Play is deeply desired: Rats will do work and press levers for chances to play together, as they would for morphine; they even laugh (at ultrasonic frequencies). Furthermore, play activates critical genes that allows the upper brain to mature.

Among mammals, we are the ultimate player. We enjoy a far longer childhood than most, and play is boosted by our bigger brains, allowing us to develop sophisticated forms, from chess to escape rooms. Panksepp later discovered that medication for attention deficit disorder acted on neurochemical routes heavily implicated in the play circuit. This resonated ominously with accounts from parents, who told how, as their child lost their antisocial behavior, they also lost their childlike playfulness. Before his death, Panksepp offered a warning: "Are we, through anti-play drugs […] taking something valuable away from our kids? I think we are."

WHY CAN'T YOU *TICKLE* YOURSELF?

68

SARAH-JAYNE BLAKEMORE
b. 1974

SOURCE: The paper "Why can't you tickle yourself?"
DATE: 2000
FIELD: Neuropsychology

Sarah-Jayne Blakemore is a professor of cognitive neuroscience at University College London whose interests include the adolescent brain and the neuroscience of education. This quote is the title of an early influential paper addressing key questions about our mind and body.

It's no easy feat to coordinate a body containing hundreds of joints, and the problem is harder once it's in motion. Just how do you keep your gaze fixed while your head bobs as you walk? To accomplish this, your brain passes around copies of your movement intentions, so they can be accounted for, instead of surprising you. (Someone applying gentle pressure to your eyelid—moving your eye without generating a movement intention—will make your vision lurch disconcertingly.) These summaries prevent us feeling shock when we absentmindedly brush our face when adjusting a hat, and they are why we can't tickle ourselves—our brain is too prepared for what's to come.

Blakemore collaborated with Chris Frith, a researcher who suspected schizophrenia involved a problem in managing intentions. They confirmed that people with schizophrenia find self-tickling just as enjoyable and intense as tickling by others, suggesting that they are missing or misreading the movement intention. This explanation begins to make sense of the wide variety of symptoms described by schizophrenic people, including the sense that manifesting emotions do not belong to them, or believing their actions are caused by alien forces. In this way, a tickling task gave insight into one of the most troubling mental illnesses.

Sometimes I wake up in the morning before going off to a shoot, and I think, I can't do this. I'm a fraud.

69

KATE WINSLET
b. 1975

SOURCE: *Interview Magazine*
DATE: 2000
FIELD: Identity

Kate Winslet is an acclaimed English actor, known for lead roles in movie such as *Iris*, *Eternal Sunshine of the Spotless Mind*, and the record-breaking *Titanic*. She is one of the few people to have won Emmy, Grammy, and Academy awards. Yet even she wonders if she deserves her job. Say hello to imposter syndrome, a term coined by clinical psychologists Pauline Rose Clance and Suzanne Imes through their investigation of issues experienced by high-achieving women. Their research suggested that the roots of the syndrome could be traced to childhood: being in the shadow of a smarter sibling, or the "perfect daughter" taught that perfection should come effortlessly, always. We now know that these feelings of fraudulence can happen to anyone, and some data suggests that men are affected almost as often as women.

These feelings can be exacerbated by organizational culture. When excellence is gendered—the *real* engineers are men—then women are likely to scrutinize their competence more harshly. What's more, workplaces with a highly collectivist culture tend to punish exceptionalism, hammering down any nail with the temerity to stand up: "Who does he think he is?" Yet individual psychological tendencies also play their part. If you are sensitive to criticism but find it difficult to take praise, are motivated by fear of failure, or are a perfectionist, the chances are higher you will feel an imposter. Clance now wishes that she had used the phrase "imposter experience"; the term "syndrome" suggests an abnormal affliction, but it's something anyone can go through. Even Kate.

It may be difficult to
learn from our mistakes.

70

DIANE F. HALPERN
b. 1947

SOURCE: *Thought and Knowledge: An Introduction to Critical Thinking*
DATE: 2002
FIELD: Decision-making

Diane F. Halpern is a world expert on critical thinking, and a researcher and developer of tests and training. So why the pessimism in this quote? Halpern alludes to the hindsight bias, a tendency first explored by Baruch Fischhoff and Ruth Beyth. On the eve of US president Richard Nixon's 1972 visit to China, they asked participants to estimate the likelihood of certain outcomes, such as a presidential meeting with Mao Zedong. One week after the visit, when asked to recall their original estimates, participants produced biased answers, colored by what had actually occurred. It was hard to step outside of the current reality and see how things might have looked in the past. Whatever happened was a foregone conclusion; Fischoff and Beyth call this a "knew it all along" attitude.

Halpern points out that you are most likely to notice the hindsight bias in action when you talk to friends or family about a mishap—a relationship gone wrong, a trip or purchase that disappointed. You will sometimes notice how they seem disproportionately certain that, given the facts, you really should have seen it coming. In our societies, citizens castigate parole boards as blunderers when they release an inmate who goes on to kill, and governments as fools for policies that have unwanted effects. From where we stand, the consequences seem obvious. Halpern laments that we can't fully rid ourselves of such biases, but we can minimize their impact, by arming ourselves with critical thinking skills. In most cases the first and biggest step is to be aware of the bias in the first place.

Memory's vices are also its virtues, elements of a bridge across time that allows us to link the mind with the world

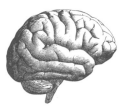

71

DANIEL SCHACTER
b. 1952

SOURCE: *The Seven Sins of Memory: How the Mind Forgets and Remembers*
DATE: 2002
FIELD: Memory

When our memory betrays us, it seems evidence that we're cursed with a badly-designed system of remembering. Daniel Schacter, however, has spent a lifetime researching memory, and he believes that its slips actually reveal the ways in which it works well. Take transience, how memories weaken over time. Would we want our breakfast from seven years ago to hover in our mind as strongly as the events of yesterday? Similarly, it's frustrating when a specific name—often one you've not recently used—refuses to come to mind. Yet, when a colleague enters the room, who would want the names of every similar-looking acquaintance to rush into mind? Memory tries not to bother us with what's ordinarily irrelevant.

The most distressing sin is persistence, bothersome memories we would prefer to forget. This can range from anxious rumination to full-blown post-traumatic stress disorder (PTSD). Yet there are reasons why bad things stick. You don't remember breakfast from seven years ago, but you might if it had made you immediately ill. Our memory system is designed to be extremely responsive to emotional experiences, in order to keep us safe.

Schacter also investigates our worrying tendency to rewrite our past to fit with our current beliefs. While this may seem Orwellian, there are benefits. For example, it helps us develop a coherent life narrative and rationalize away disappointment (see page 165). All in all, Schacter argues that these sins may be annoying to experience, but they illustrate a helpful memory system worthy of admiration.

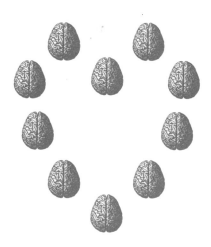

MY THEORY IS THAT THE FEMALE BRAIN IS
PREDOMINANTLY HARD-WIRED FOR EMPATHY,
AND THAT THE MALE BRAIN IS PREDOMINANTLY
HARD-WIRED FOR UNDERSTANDING AND BUILDING SYSTEMS.

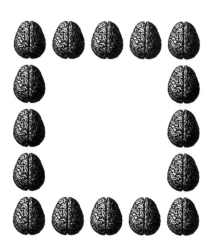

SIMON BARON-COHEN
b. 1958

SOURCE: "They Just Can't Help It," *The Guardian*
DATE: 2003
FIELD: Neuropsychology

Simon Baron-Cohen is a Cambridge professor of developmental psychopathology who believes humans relate to the world in two main ways: by focusing more on people or on ideas and objects. Your sex does not determine this, but it does have a steering effect. It might be said that this tallies with a world where women are commonly nurses and men engineers; men have their solitary pottering sheds, women get-togethers. Are these innate differences, rather than being socialized, or mere stereotypes? Enter the dissenters, such as Cordelia Fine, a critic of "neurosexism" who has debated Baron-Cohen through books, reviews, and counterreviews.

The debate focuses on differences in children. Research indicates that girls from age seven are quicker to read nonverbal communication and more likely to attribute harm to bluntly phrased speech. Meanwhile, boys are more self-centered, more aggressive, and share less. Admittedly, such children have already been exposed to gendered concepts. At 1 year old, infant girls show more sympathy when viewing someone in distress. One-year-old boys, in contrast to girls, prefer to watch movies involving cars rather than a person's face. This could be accounted for by evidence that parents treat even infant boys and girls differently. Now a major front is the study of newborns, with studies indicating that girls look longer at faces than boys do, while boys are more apt to look longer at a mechanical mobile than girls are—and that these effects are mediated by hormone levels distributed differently in the sexes. Still, Fine and other neurocritics have pounced on problems with this research. It seems the only point of current agreement is that there are small early differences, but culture plays some role in magnifying whatever is innate.

It will
take time to
restore chaos
and order.

73

GEORGE W. BUSH
b. 1946

SOURCE: C-SPAN
DATE: 2003
FIELD: Language

The divisive 43rd president of the United States, George W. Bush launched the War on Terror and a neoconservative foreign policy. Beyond his political legacy, he will be remembered for "Bushisms," volumes-worth of verbal slipups that are amusing coming from the leader of the free world. Psycholinguists love to catalog speech errors: We make anticipations, using a sound too early, such as Ted Kennedy's "encourage the breast and brightest." A perseveration is getting stuck on an old sound, like "black bloxes."

This isn't idle butterfly collecting; these errors are clues about our linguistic minds. Researchers David Fay and Anne Cutler studied the organization of our mental lexicon. If it was optimized for speaking, it should be like a thesaurus. With related words grouped together, when you stumbled for a word and missed you should grab a conceptual relative, making minor mistakes like "a fool and his money are soon detached." Yet we don't see these kinds of spontaneous errors. Instead, we see malapropisms, the substitution of a similar-sounding but typically nonsensical word—named after Mrs. Malaprop from Richard Sheridan's comedy *The Rivals* who would substitute "allegory" with "alligator," or "epitaph" for "epithet."

To Fay and Cutler, this suggests that our lexicon groups similar-sounding words together to optimize the job of hearing, allowing us to quickly tell between different possibilities when listening under noisy conditions. Hearing is hard, so we optimize for it, and speech occasionally pays the price.

In most collectivist cultures [...] the word no is seldom used, because saying "no" is a confrontation.

74

GEERT HOFSTEDE
b. 1928

SOURCE: *Culture and Organizations: Software of the Mind*
DATE: 2004
FIELD: Social psychology

Dutch psychologist Geert Hofstede is a leader in understanding cultural differences. Instead of treating national cultures as idiosyncratic and unique, Hofstede discovered much of their difference came down to where they stood on a small number of dimensions. One is power distance, the willingness of those at the bottom to tolerate having a smaller say in their society. You can see this in preferences for respectful children rather than independent ones, and in workplaces where subordinates prefer instruction to consultation. In cultures high on uncertainty avoidance, meanwhile, everyone needs to agree on what is true and acceptable, with clear codes of behavior, whereas other cultures rely on informal norms and are comfortable with strangers.

More masculine societies have strong gender roles—boys don't cry, girls don't fight, and in the family father deals with facts and mother with feelings. A feminine one prioritizes home–life balance, but may treat high-flyers with suspicion, as epitomized in the Nordic countries. Some cultures are oriented toward how things were in the past, honoring traditions and valuing consistency; others are more pragmatic and willing to change now to adapt to tomorrow. Cultures may differ in how much they prize indulgence versus restraint.

The quote opposite refers to the final dimension of collectivism: individualism. In some societies people live in strong ingroups, like tribes or extended families, while others are atomized, with weak ties between people. Knowing this—and that in collectivist cultures like Japan, a "yes" may only mean "yes, I heard you"—has helped many people navigate this ever-more global world.

Are all
smiles the
same?

75

PAUL EKMAN
b. 1934

SOURCE: *Emotions Revealed: Recognizing Faces and Feelings to Improve Communication and Emotional Life*
DATE: 2004
FIELD: Emotion

If anyone would know the answer to the question opposite, it's Paul Ekman. Ekman's early cross-cultural work on facial expressions led to the development of the idea of at least six basic emotions—fear, anger, disgust, surprise, sadness, and joy—that are universal to humanity, and which have evolved for distinct purposes. We become angry so we can tackle injustices, when someone takes a greedy share of the fruit or threatens your kin. Expressions of fear signal danger, and sadness signals need for support. These emotions may seem familiar to moviegoers, as they are the archetypes Pixar used in its movie *Inside Out*. In a recent poll 80 percent of emotion researchers stated a belief that, as per Ekman's view, emotions are prewired and universal, even if they differ on the details.

Ekman now devotes himself to understanding micro expressions, tiny flashes of emotion that peek out, even when we hope to conceal them. He began this quest after fielding a sober question from a psychiatric student: How could they trust a suicide risk patient when they say they feel better and want to be released? By forensically studying video, sometimes in slow motion, he realized the answer was there, dancing across the face. His science has been used by the police, FBI, and CIA, as well as lawyers and even poker players. Ekman has been loosely immortalized in television too: He acted as a scientific advisor on the show *Lie to Me*, and its main character is a fictionalized take on Ekman himself. A smile can conceal many emotions, but to tell them apart needs an expert eye.

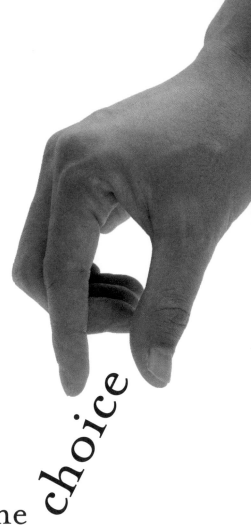

The fact that some **choice** is good doesn't necessarily mean that **more choice** is better.

76

BARRY SCHWARTZ
b. 1946

SOURCE: *The Paradox of Choice: Why More Is Less*
DATE: 2005
FIELD: Decision-making

Barry Schwartz is the Cassandra of choice. He rebuffs a world that prizes options over everything: in consumer contexts, in healthcare, in lifestyles. Armed with the evidence, Schwartz shows how increasing choice has harmful consequences. Options can paralyze: as companies offer more pension schemes, the data shows overall uptake actually declines. Furthermore, they make our choices less satisfying, even unpleasant.

How, exactly? Firstly, any disappointments we have fill us with regret that we chose *this* of all options. Even if things go as planned, the knowledge that our second choice had other benefits can eat away at our pleasure. When we have not just three, but three hundred wedding cakes to choose from, we expect the result to be outstanding—but it rarely is. Who's to blame? The foolish chooser, every time.

Beyond consumer issues, consider the ill, worried patient with the additional pressure of choosing their treatment, thanks to "patient autonomy." Or the parent at sports day zoning out to decide whether to send that nagging email, thanks to always-on technology. Or young people given a plethora of ways to define their identity—but they need to get it right. Schwartz believes choice may be a contributor to suicide and depression. On a personal level, one way to reduce choice is to have hard-and-fast rules for life: never be unfaithful, always buy the second-cheapest Italian red. As excess choice is a consequence of excess wealth, Schwartz cheers on global economic redistribution, so we can produce the right level of choice for everyone.

BECOMING

IS BETTER

THAN BEING.

77

CAROL DWECK
b. 1946

SOURCE: *Mindset*
DATE: 2006
FIELD: Creativity and Potential

Carol Dweck's research on "growth mindset" began a movement in education. The term refers to holding the view that intelligence is malleable and improvable, in contrast with a fixed mindset, which considers it innate. Dweck showed that a growth mindset helped schoolchildren perform better. More surprisingly, an intervention as simple as praising a child for making effort (rather than for being smart) could instill this mindset, producing marked improvement in their performance and sticking power. Before long, the mindset philosophy was adopted into teacher training, first in America, then the wider world.

However, there are caveats to this success story. Dweck's ideas can be misused—given lip service to make a school look progressive, or used as a pretext for teachers promoting their "just buck up" philosophy. Furthermore, the science has been challenged, especially the huge effects found in the original study, although Dweck points out there are multiple large-scale investigations linking mindset to school academic achievement.

It's also important to understand what parts of the intervention actually matter. It involves a message about bettering yourself through making an effort, and there is no doubt this improves life outcomes—the data on conscientious people (see page 163) is very clear. Yet the mindset philosophy adds the specific claim that intelligence is very malleable—a claim not supported by evidence. You can become more skilled, more informed, and, with work, improve your temperament. Perhaps we should ask young people to focus on these things, rather than a trait over which they have little influence.

It seems that
it's absolutely true that
"laugh and the whole
world laughs with you."

78

SOPHIE SCOTT
b. 1966

SOURCE: "Ha ha ha: Did that make you smile?" *NBCnews.com*
DATE: 2006
FIELD: Emotion

Sophie Scott, deputy director of the Institute of Cognitive Neuroscience in London and a lecturer for the Royal Society Christmas lectures, somehow finds time to moonlight as a stand-up comic. It's no random hobby; Scott is a world expert in the science of laughter. There is evidence of laughter in species including rats (see page 139), and it seems to have old, animal roots in humans too. When we laugh, we lose control of our breathing apparatus, in contrast to its measured use in speech, and the sounds we make are acoustically close enough to animal sounds that, slowed down, they become indistinguishable. It can seize the whole body—as comedian Keegan-Michael Key illustrates with abandon on his TV show, lamenting, "It's out of the question for me to laugh sitting still."

Laughing is extremely contagious. We laugh more in company, only partly because of social convention. Hearing laughter actually activates motor areas of the brain, preparing our face muscles and forcing at least an involuntary twitch of the mouth, if not full-on cackling. This seems to be because laughter is a bonding activity, and the first laugh is a cue to others that it's time to relax and start building more positive ties with each other. Even babies in unfamiliar situations are reassured if their caregiver laughs. Meanwhile people with conditions like autism aren't swept up by these contagious effects and are more likely to miss out on the joke. Understanding the science of the snigger may help us make sense of what binds and divides us.

Much of the systematic variation in personality can be reduced to scores along five dimensions (the "Big Five")

Agreeableness,

Neuroticism,

Extraversion,

Conscientiousness,

and Openness.

DANIEL NETTLE
b. 1970

SOURCE: *Personality: What Makes You the Way You Are?*
DATE: 2007
FIELD: Psychometrics

Personality assessments come in every flavor, whether you want to know your personality color or your Myers-Briggs type, whether an "INFP" or an "ESTJ." However, as British psychologist Daniel Nettle notes, the evidence is clear: There is one model to rule them all.

The Big Five are Openness to Experience (creativity and interest in esthetics), Conscientiousness (tidiness and industriousness), Extraversion (sensation seeking and gregariousness), Agreeableness (compassion and deference toward others) and Neuroticism (sensitivity to negativity). The Big Five have a distinguished pedigree, with origins in a questionnaire designed by the USA's first professor of psychology, James Cattell, and developed over the years down to these remarkably robust factors. Paul Costa and Robert McCrea consider the model as a "Christmas tree" on which all the varied replicable findings on personality can hang together.

One angle added by modern researchers like Nettle is an evolutionary explanation for why we vary in these traits at all. If conscientiousness is useful—which it is, predicting work success, longer life, and staying out of prison—why aren't we all evolved to be maximally conscientious? Firstly, because extremes in personality tend to be pathological, both the person with no impulse control and the perfectionist paralyzed by failure. Secondly, different strategies may be useful in different generations—a time of order or a time of chaos—so the genome keeps variety tucked inside it ready to reap rewards. So human personality, and the Big Five, tell us something about the world we inhabited in the past, and may again in the future.

Bad things don't affect us as profoundly as we expect them to. That's true of good things, too.

80

DANIEL GILBERT
b. 1957

SOURCE: "The Smiling Professor," *New York Times*
DATE: 2008
FIELD: Perception and biases

Despite his Harvard nickname, "Professor Happiness," Dan Gilbert has experienced rough times. It was during a particularly rough one, involving divorce and death, that he noticed how even this was not as devastating as he would have thought. Fascinated by optical illusions as a boy, he came to wonder if there were also illusions of happiness. This led him to cofound the field of affective forecasting, exploring whether we can predict how we'll feel in the future.

The answer is, not very well. We overestimate both the happiness produced by a lottery win and the misery of going blind. This is partly because it's simply hard to forecast future internal states, like accepting you will want cookies later, even though you're currently shopping on a full stomach. Also, we underestimate how quickly we boomerang back to our baseline level of happiness. We are able to rationalize situations away, finding silver linings in redundancies or relationships that end. (This turns out to be difficult for people with clinical depression, who are more likely to stay locked in to old, unproductive ways of seeing the world.) Our emotion system seems to have a homeostatic quality, like a thermostat keeping temperature from straying to extremes: We need to reset, so we can be affected by new events in the environment. Emotions are a signal of novelty, so once we hit a new normal, we have to recalibrate. In Gilbert's words, we possess a "psychological immune system" that makes sure we can react to the next day as... just another day.

Every brain has a story
and this is mine.

81

JILL BOLTE TAYLOR
b. 1959

SOURCE: *My Stroke of Insight: A Brain Scientist's Personal Journey*
DATE: 2009
FIELD: Neuropsychology

On December 10, 1996, Jill Bolte Taylor was alone working from home when a caustic pain in her head began to take grip. She was experiencing a stroke, but from the rare vantage point of a neuroanatomist who researched the brain in daily life. She noted how the stroke knocked out the control and organization functions in her left hemisphere; hour after hour she lost the ability to process information. Her body became alien and unfamiliar, and soon she could no longer define its boundaries—where she began and ended blurred into the surroundings. Her internal mental chatter fell away to silence.

Rather than being terrifying, the experience was profound. She felt with crystal clarity that she was part of everything, simply energy. Yet from time to time her frazzled processes rebooted, demanding that she get it together and get help. She gives a wry description of the bursts of mental commentary in her TED Talk on this event: "But I'm a very busy woman—I don't have time for a stroke!" She managed to attract help, and after a clot the size of a golf ball was removed from her brain, began a recovery process that took eight years.

She has used her experiences as an advocate for stroke recovery on behalf of the National Alliance for Mental Illness, but also for her own message: "We are energy beings connected to each other through the consciousness of our right hemisphere." It's a claim based on her deep knowledge of the nature of hemispheric differences (see page 169) and her humbling lived experience.

"No man is an island": it is the right hemisphere of the human brain that ensures that we feel part of the main

82

IAIN MCGILCHRIST
b. 1953

SOURCE: *The Master and His Emissary: The Divided Brain and the Making of the Western World*
DATE: 2009
FIELD: Neuropsychology

Left brain, right brain—many generalizations have been made about our two largely separate hemispheres, but the Scottish psychiatrist Iain McGilchrist is our foremost living expert in what that actually means. One commonly held belief is that the left hemisphere reasons while the right is creative, but this is false—both depend on processes found across the brain. Neither do we have one side for language and the other for visual information. In McGilchrist's view, based on data on neurological patients and neuroscience techniques, the "world of difference" between the hemispheres is not what they do, but how they do it.

The left brain is detail-oriented, focusing attention on things deemed as important. It tries to maximize clarity by isolating components and stripping away the irrelevant, to make predictions and act successfully. Its world is a closed system of clockwork cause and effect. The right brain has the global view. It deems importance, decides on meaning, is alert, makes connections, notices context. Its world is a mass of changing, evolving, interconnected, and living things.

McGilchrist sees the right hemisphere as the fundament of our being, with the left hemisphere as a storehouse of powerful tools to aid it—in his metaphor, a master served by his emissary. He worries that our societies have become topsy-turvy in prioritizing clarity, detail, and reductionism, becoming so taken by these useful tools that we mistake them for the whole. We need the whole, the holistic approach of the right hemisphere that connects us outward and prevents us retreating into alienation.

How is it so easy to know other minds

83

REBECCA SAXE
b. 1979

SOURCE: "How We Read Each Other's Minds," TEDGlobal 2009
DATE: 2009
FIELD: Neuropsychology

Rebecca Saxe is a professor running a MIT lab and one of the World Economic Forum's young global leaders. She has developed our understanding of Theory of Mind, our ability to know what someone else wants or believes. A great illustration of this comes from the classic Sally-Anne test, created by autism researcher Uta Frith. Working with Alan Leslie and her PhD student Simon Baron-Cohen (see page 149), children of different ages were shown a story using small dolls: Sally stashes her marble in a basket, but then Anne secretly moves it to a box. Under-fours think that when Sally returns she will immediately go to the box, unable to separate the facts from Sally's mental state. Saxe took this paradigm and added a moral spin—and sandwiches. If a doll mistakenly eats another's sandwich due to a mix-up, are they to blame? Young kids say yes, older ones recognize that intentions should be taken into account.

Using brain imaging techniques, Saxe identified the brain area active in these moral judgments about intention, the right temporoparietal junction. Using a technique called transcranial magnetic stimulation, which can temporarily disrupt brain activity, Saxe showed it's possible to change adult participants' responses on a version of this task. By zapping their brains, they were rendered more judgmental toward someone whose innocent actions had caused harm. As scary as this research can sound, it's valuable in developing our understanding of conditions like autism, where the difficulty of knowing the minds of others is a key deficit, making it hard to handle more nuanced social situations.

Staying vulnerable

is a risk we have to take

if we want to experience

connection.

84

BRENÉ BROWN
b. 1965

SOURCE: *The Gifts of Imperfection: Let Go of Who You Think You're Supposed to Be and Embrace Who You Are*
DATE: 2010
FIELD: Well-being

Brené Brown is a professor of social work at the University of Houston who had an epiphany while trying to understand human connection. Again and again her informants would go off-track, confessing all the things that prevented them from connecting, and again and again they originated in a feeling of shame. Through thousands of pieces of data from years of interviews and focus groups, Brown built a comprehensive picture of the emotion. Guilt is feeling bad about something you've done, but shame is a feeling about who you are, of being unworthy of connection. It digs deeper into your identity, and correlates with depression, aggression, and addiction. What to do about this alienating feeling?

Some of Brown's informants had an answer: the way through was by facing vulnerability. Uncertainty, risk, and emotional exposure were the conditions from which shame could spring, but by having the courage to embrace them wholeheartedly, the emotion could find no handhold. As someone who prided themselves on staying in control, Brown was shook by the notion that this could be harming her, which took her to emotional breakdown, and breakthrough. You can find this message foreshadowed in the work of several 20th-century psychotherapists (see page 63), and thanks to Brown's frank charisma it has found its way to a much larger audience. Her writings are aimed chiefly at personal change, but her work also has policy implications, such as providing better teacher training on classroom control to discourage the use of shaming as a blunt if effective instrument, as this can leave lasting wounds in a child's notion of its worth as a learner.

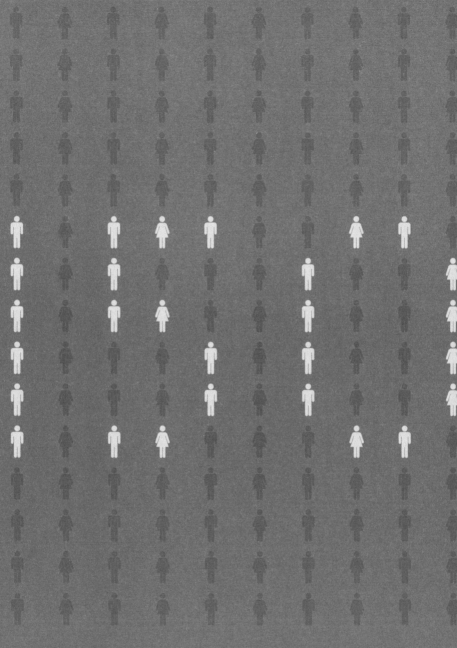

is the number of people you can have a relationship with involving trust and obligation.

85

ROBIN DUNBAR
b. 1947

SOURCE: The interview "My Bright Idea: Robin Dunbar"
DATE: 2010
FIELD: Human universals

Sociologists and anthropologists have studied human social groups for more than a century. However, we had to wait for an evolutionary psychologist to identify the upper limit of the social group. Robin Dunbar had been playing around with data on mammal social group size and the volume of their brain. He found there was a relationship between the two, and by carrying it forward from rats and monkeys to the human species, Dunbar arrived at a number of around 150. Intrigued, he looked for corroboration, and found that hunter-gatherer societies tend to max out at 150 people. Villages as surveyed in the Domesday Book at the start of Norman England? 150. The average village size in the 18th century? 150. Clearly, it's possible to build large networks of acquaintances—the number of an individual's friends on Facebook can run into the thousands. Yet, 150 seems to be the stable state for relationships that involve trust and interdependence, feeling responsible for someone's well-being, and they for yours.

One likely reason for our bigger brains is the need to handle large amounts of social information. We are built socially, and we solve problems—from bringing down a mammoth to putting up a bridge—through coordinated action. Dunbar's number reflects this: "The way in which our social world is constructed is part and parcel of our biological inheritance." Times have changed. Our relationships used to be localized in tribes or villages. Now we fill up our number with people across the world, asynchronously via online chat, but don't know our neighbors. Time will tell if this will be a problem for our social species.

Small boys are not Freudians but they know they have their own beanstalk; and that it takes them away from life at home.

86

ADAM PHILLIPS
b. 1954

SOURCE: *On Balance*
DATE: 2010
FIELD: Therapy

With more than eighteen books to his name and responsibility for the Penguin Modern Classics translations of Freud, Adam Phillips is one of the most preeminent modern psychoanalysts. Yet he takes it lightly, suggesting that when people feel unwell, they have many options—aromatherapy or hang-gliding might also do the trick. For Phillips, analysis is a set of stories that can help us sometimes, nothing more.

Here, he storifies the psychoanalytic theme that has penetrated farthest: sex. Previously ignored or pathologized, Sigmund Freud (see page 29) was the first to place the sex drive as central to being human. He forced us to admit that sex is often on our minds, and a source of pleasure we can access even at an early age through self-touch and imagination. It's a prime motivator, and repressing it is likely to cause problems.

That's not to say there are no dangers in sex, even consensual sex. There is a movement to recognize sex addiction as comparable to dependence on drugs and alcohol. Consumption of online pornography also raises concerns, and the neuroscientist Norman Doidge fears it can permanently warp the libido. He hypothesizes that browsing through different types of pornography to look for a hit can expose the user to fetishes and desires laid down in the brain during early sexual development—a wholly Freudian idea. Feeding these through orgasm after orgasm can build these deep-rooted networks until they crush out any competing sexual appetites. So whether you grow up with a beanstalk or a bean, enjoy where it takes you, but be mindful it does not become your master.

Every point on the body's surface has a corresponding point in the brain.

87

V. S. RAMACHANDRAN
b. 1951

SOURCE: "V. S. Ramachandran's Tales of the 'Tell-Tale Brain,'" NPR
DATE: 2011
FIELD: Neuropsychology

Vilayanur Subramanian Ramachandran is among our most inventive neuroscientists. In this quote, he describes the discovery by pioneering neurologist Wilder Penfield (see page 119) that our brain's surface carries maps of our body, one for registering sensations, and one for guiding movement. Each map proceeds from foot to head, with larger areas where sensitivity is needed—for instance the fingers, face, and tongue—a strange-shaped miniature man in the brain, a "cortical homunculus."

Ramachandran drew on this knowledge to tackle the puzzle of phantom limb, a common condition following the loss of a limb. The patient feels unpleasant sensations from where the leg or arm once was—itches, clenching, or the discomfort of a permanently awkward position.

Ramachandran thought that when the limb's area of the sensation map had gone silent, other neighboring areas might have claimed the territory. By recreating arm sensations in an amputee by stroking areas of their face (on the brain map, this neighbors the arm), he showed this was plausible. Since then, he and others have investigated how these remapped connections might go awry, leading minor sensations to be read as displaced pain.

The knowledge that the brain maps can change gave Ramachandran an unusual idea for treating phantom cramps. Using a mirror to project the person's good limb to where the missing one would be, they could "see" it move again, waking up the abandoned part of the movement homunculus. After a period of such training, the phantom limb could be "moved" into a comfortable position.

THE GORILLA WAS INVISIBLE.

DANIEL SIMONS
b. 1969

SOURCE: The Invisible Gorilla website
DATE: 2011
FIELD: Perceptions and biases

Daniel Simons' Illinois Visual Cognition Laboratory offers the chance to take their landmark experiment yourself—online at theinvisiblegorilla.com. If you can, have a go, before the spoilers. The experiment involves watching a video of people playing ball and counting the number of passes made between certain players. Once the task ends, your attention is drawn to a strange fact: A gorilla-suited person had walked right through the game, even stopping to beat their chest when at the center of the screen. Half of participants don't notice the gorilla. Did you?

The experiment demonstrates inattentional blindness, a failure to perceive something because you put your attention elsewhere. This is the downside of the powers of attention first explored by William James (see page 25). It still seems surprising the gorilla could be invisible while posing brazenly at center stage. Yet the science suggests that's where we can be most blinded, if preoccupied elsewhere. Our visual attention loves the center so much that to divert focus away means our brain has to inhibit—block—whatever is happening there. This is why things can disappear when they're right in front of your nose.

Inattentional blindness can get us in trouble: Simons gives the example of scanning the rows of cinema seating to search for a free place, and afterward being berated by a friend who can't understand why you ignored them. It can also be dangerous, if we are scanning the road ahead for the yellow corvette that cut us up earlier. Yet to some extent it's inevitable: We see what we need to see.

DON'T THINK OF  INTROVERSION AS SOMETHING THAT NEEDS TO BE CURED.

89

SUSAN CAIN
b. 1968

SOURCE: *Quiet: The Power of Introverts in a World That Can't Stop Talking*
DATE: 2012
FIELD: Psychometrics

Susan Cain was a successful corporate lawyer in a culture that didn't understand or include her. In an earlier generation the problem would have been gender. Yet she encountered another kind of obstacle, as one of many "second-class citizens with gigantic amounts of untapped talent"—she is an introvert. Cain decided it was high time they had an advocate.

In her writing and talks, Cain points out that extroverts claim space, are gregarious, and project their energy out. This means that the world ends up being designed around their needs. Whether in the jostling workplace or the status cauldron of the schoolyard, introverts either fade out or learn to fake it and fight on extrovert terms. Faking it is emotionally draining, and introverts are more likely to burn out at work (see page 103). Instead, we should celebrate what an introvert can offer.

Cain points out creative breakthroughs don't all come in a bustling bullpen, but through musing, deep thought, and solo time—the natural niche of the introvert. They can be quite effectively social, focusing more on the duties of a listener and receiving rather than projecting in interactions. We shouldn't assume that extroverts are living life more fully. Introverts are more sensitive to sensation, meaning that they are squeezing the fullest from even quiet experiences, like walking along a quiet lane at dusk; the highly extrovert may need rollercoasters and thumping bass to get the same satisfaction. With those facts in mind, Cain entreats us to see introversion not as a problem but as a distinctive and valuable flavor of humanity.

You can do what you decide to do—but you cannot decide what you will decide to do.

90

SAM HARRIS
b. 1967

SOURCE: *Free Will*
DATE: 2012
FIELD: Existentialism

The neuroscientist Sam Harris is an influential podcaster, one of the "four horsemen" of New Atheism, and a meditation practitioner with no belief in free will. "If you pay attention to your inner life," he says, "you will see that the emergence of choices, efforts, and intentions is a fundamentally mysterious process." You can decide to start your diet today, but not know exactly why it just *felt* right. So where's the freedom?

Harris also promotes Benjamin Libet's research concerning when decisions happen. This appears to show that, by the time you are consciously aware of choosing an action, your brain has already prepared it—the choosing was an illusion. While Libet's work made a splash, its conclusions have been contested—for instance, it assumes that the point where a choice is "experienced" consciously is the only one where free choice could operate.

It's true that any sequence of events can be dissected and each step defined either as determined (so not free) or random (also not free). So a zoomed-in, reductionist (and left-brained—see page 169) perspective rules out free will, but does that miss the picture? As an analogy, consider a pianist playing a complex piece. Her attention is racing ahead in the score, which means the key-strikes needed now must be automatic—the playing out of a program. Yet she is also the programmer who built and set it in motion. This thorniest of problems deserves to be taken seriously by psychologists, especially as belief in free will appears to be associated with happiness and life success.

Laziness is built deep into our nature.

91

DANIEL KAHNEMAN
b. 1934

SOURCE: *Thinking, Fast and Slow*
DATE: 2012
FIELD: Decision-making

With the late Amos Tversky, Israeli-American psychologist Daniel Kahneman transformed our understanding of decision-making and thought. Before them, the scientific impulse was to treat people as rational actors who use cost–benefit analysis to maximize their personal advantage. Yet, as Kahneman writes in *Thinking, Fast and Slow*, "It is self-evident that people are neither fully rational nor completely selfish." The book describes two mental routes: the considered, slower "System 2"; and a nimble and automatic "System 1," which actually does most of the work. We revert to System 2 only when necessary: It does the parking in a tight space, whereas 1 is what spends the hour coasting along an open road.

In decision-making, System 2 does resemble something like a "rational actor" approach. Yet in practice most choices are punted to System 1, which uses heuristics—rules of thumb that work well enough in most cases. These include the availability heuristic ("as this feels familiar, it must be common") and the representativeness heuristic ("this looks right, so it is right"). The latter was the subject of Tversky and Kahneman's 1974 landmark paper, which asked participants to estimate whether "Linda"—an activist concerned with social justice—is more likely to be: a) a bank teller; or b) a bank teller active in the feminist movement. The heuristic guides people to the representative option b), even though a) must be at least as likely or more, as it contains b) within it. This work transformed psychology and launched a new field of behavioral economics, leading Kahneman to a Nobel Prize in 2002.

Well-being, not happiness, is the topic of positive psychology.

92

MARTIN SELIGMAN
b. 1942

SOURCE: *Flourish: A Visionary New Understanding of Happiness and Well-being*
DATE: 2012
FIELD: Well-being

Martin Seligman is one of the major architects of the positive psychology movement. You could say he wrote the book on it: *Character Strengths and Virtues* was written to be a positive version of the psychiatric manual of mental illness, listing strengths instead of pathologies. Positive psychology, like humanistic psychology before it, is an attempt to reframe the field. As Seligman comments, "Beauty is not just the absence of ugliness, bravery is not just the absence of cowardice, and well-being is not just the absence of misery—it's the presence of real things." However, as positive psychology grew, its message became garbled; to many it was simply the pursuit of happiness. Pursuing this hedonistic philosophy could lead us to be like the inhabitants of Aldous Huxley's dystopian *Brave New World*, constantly soothed by mood-lifting drugs, or those of Mike Judge's *Idiocracy*, sated by television.

For Seligman, these are not stars to set our sights on. He wrote *Flourish* to articulate an alternative: not hedonia but eudemonia, the prosperous good life, being well, not merely happy. This depended on "PERMA": Positive emotion, Engagement (Csíkszentmihályi's flow states; see page 113), Relationships, Meaning, and Accomplishment. Seligman has years of research showing the impact of these factors. One unexpected but robust finding is that the best way to increase well-being, and lift yourself from depression, is to do something good for somebody else. These generous acts can even have a ripple effect, starting a virtuous circle of further benevolence. A well-lived life is the opposite of a soporific daze: It's one where we participate in transforming the world.

My experiment had worked. The human brain is capable of change.

93

BARBARA ARROWSMITH-YOUNG
b. 1951

SOURCE: "The Woman Who Changed Her Brain," TEDxToronto
DATE: 2013
FIELD: Neuropsychology

Barbara Arrowsmith-Young had lived with learning difficulties all her life. Struggling to understand abstractions or navigate social situations, she found her condition so debilitating she attempted suicide. Her study of psychology threw her a lifeline.

In writings by the great Russian neuropsychologist Alexander Luria, she discovered a kindred spirit, a brain-injured soldier whose condition mirrored hers, right down to a particular difficulty in reading clock faces. He'd had to endure it, but did she? Her reading had revealed studies showing remarkable brain growth in rats when they were placed in enriched environments with challenging activities. She decided to follow suit by training her brain.

Grueling practice on basic mental tasks—she began with clocks, adding more hands when it became too easy—seemed to fundamentally transform her thinking. She now runs programs for people with learning difficulties; enrolling involves devoting at least half of each school day to these effortful processing tasks. Some children appear to thrive as she did, able finally to follow movies and enjoy complex interactions. Yet these anecdotal reports may simply reflect improvements that would have happened anyway, and to date there have been no fully controlled studies to say otherwise. In general, the investigations to date of commercial "brain training" programs do not support claims of benefits that go well beyond improvement on the practiced tasks. More than anything, we can hope Arrowsmith-Young's is the real deal—but the evidence will have the final say.

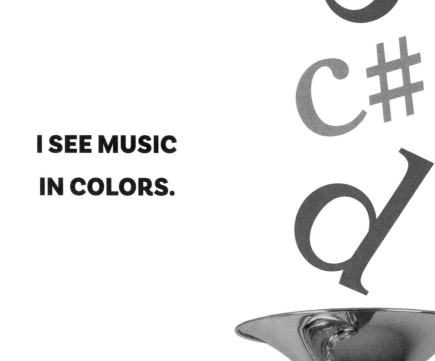

I SEE MUSIC
IN COLORS.

94

MARY J. BLIGE
b. 1971

SOURCE: *LA Confidential Magazine*
DATE: 2013
FIELD: Perception

Mary J. Blige, the Grammy Award-winning singer from New York, isn't the only one. A swathe of artists and musicians experience synesthesia, a condition where certain kinds of perception are accompanied by an extra layer of experience, such as colors accompanying musical tones. From Lorde to Liszt ("Please, gentlemen, a little bluer, if you please!" Liszt would say), Billy Joel to Duke Ellington ("If Harry Carney is playing, D is dark blue burlap," Ellington explained), many synesthetes use art to express their unique perspectives.

Synesthesia isn't confined to music: there are sixty or more variants, one of the most common being perceiving numbers or letters accompanied by color (for the novelist Vladimir Nabokov, "m" was "a fold of pink flannel"). For some people, the mention of a number conjures it up visually in certain locations in space, creating number maps or ladders. As well as artistic expression, some evidence ties synesthesia to memory skills, noted first by the Russian neuropsychologist Alexander Luria in his case study of "III," the mnemonicist who experienced five forms of synesthesia.

Later, the 1989 publication of *Synesthesia: A Union of the Senses* by Richard Cytowick helped pull scientific focus back onto the condition, which we now know affects around four percent of people. Explanations include information leaking from one brain sensory area to another, or that the meaning associated with things we perceive triggers further sensory associations (the "ideasthesia" theory). It's likely that we have all experienced it once as infants. Expert Maureen Seaberg explains that as we age, "a pruning process goes on in the normal population but synesthetes stay hyper-interconnected."

**The negative
screams at you
but the positive
only whispers.**

95

BARBARA FREDRICKSON
b. 1964

SOURCE: *Love 2.0: How Our Supreme Emotion Affects Everything We Feel, Think, Do, and Become*
DATE: 2013
FIELD: Creativity and potential

Barbara Frederickson, a social psychologist based at the University of North Carolina, is the grand dame of positivity. The quote refers to her highly cited and shared study that suggests living a flourishing life requires three positive emotional experiences for every negative one. Frederickson has since retreated from this precise numerical claim, but she still sticks to the central point: We need a preponderance of positivity in our lives to flourish.

As loud as the bad can be, Frederickson is most fascinated by the good. Her "broaden and build" theory outlines the longer-term benefits of positive emotion. When we are stressed and worried, we focus on solving immediate issues—the extreme responses of fight or flight, or forcing yourself to get that spreadsheet sent tonight, come what may. In contrast, positive emotions switch us into an exploratory mode, which pays off in a variety of ways. Curiosity about the unknown leads us to expanding our knowledge. Play and adventure help us become stronger and more competent. Expanding our social horizons leads to new or deeper friendships. By broadening our horizons now, we build for ourselves a better tomorrow.

Frederickson's research also investigates the effect of positivity on the body, which suggests that positive states like happiness or relaxation actually counteract the negative cardiovascular changes produced by stress, something she terms the undoing effect. So seeking out positive experiences helps us to be healthier, more skilled, more social, and smarter.

Evil behavior results
not just from evil people
but also ordinary people
in bad contexts.

96

LASANA HARRIS
b. 1981

SOURCE: The article "Why Economic, Health, Legal, and Immigration Policy Should Consider Dehumanization"
DATE: 2014
FIELD: Social psychology

Lasana Harris is a London-based researcher on the brain science of social thinking and dehumanization. Dehumanization has long interested psychologists, who often look at how people talk about out-group members— as vermin, cockroaches, or trash. Brain imaging techniques allow us to understand how people see them, too. When we perceive something, we quickly determine whether we can socially interact with it. If so, it activates specific social areas in the brain in a process called person perception. Yet not everyone counts as a person: These brain regions are more weakly activated when seeing people from extremely marginalized groups like the homeless. So dehumanization manifests in how we see the world.

What determines when we see personhood? It can't be locked in; in the past, living without a fixed abode was far more common and relatively unstigmatized. It's a product of the forces of language and rhetoric—if you hear "vermin" long enough you start to perceive it.

Harris' research shows market concepts can trigger dehumanization: Sports players are seen as less person-like once they are "bought" in a fantasy league, turned from human to resource. Simply being encouraged to feel powerful encourages us to dehumanize. So the humanity in others can be obscured through language, economics, and hierarchy.

Yet when person perception kicks into gear, the data shows that it automatically generates a swell of positive feeling. Ultimately, we are a hugely social species, people born to love other people. The only question is how well we make good on that potential.

Expanding your body language—through posture, movement, and speech—makes you feel more confident and powerful, less anxious and self-absorbed, and generally more positive.

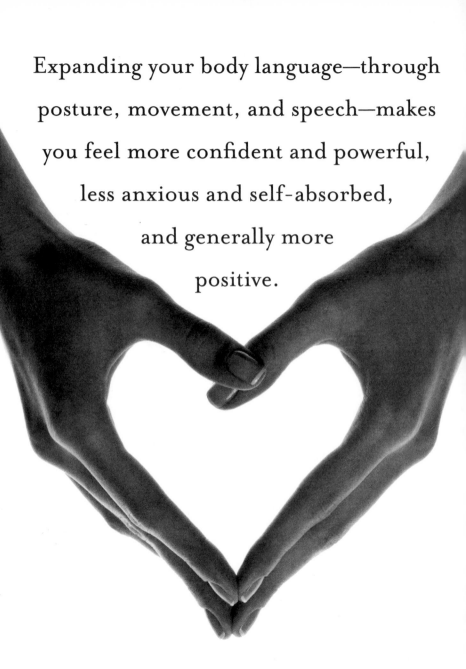

97

AMY CUDDY
b. 1972

SOURCE: *Presence: Bringing Your Boldest Self to Your Biggest Challenges*
DATE: 2015
FIELD: Creativity and potential

Following a serious head injury, Amy Cuddy was told she would never be fit to complete university. Nevertheless she became a Princeton researcher and one of the most famous figures in social psychology. As she rose, however, her field fell into discord, and her landmark finding was caught in the crosshairs.

In a TED talk watched by over 45 million viewers, Cuddy gave power posing to the world. She told how expansive physical postures like a hands-on-hips "Wonder Woman" pose led to profound effects. You will feel more powerful and take more confident decisions. Even your body will respond, through a calming drop in cortisol and more assertive testosterone. Posing for just two minutes before an interview could improve performance, "bring your true self," and change your future. The world took note.

A new movement in psychology also took note, alarmed by the dawning realization that its standard research practices were dangerously lax. Power posing's prominence made it a prime target, leading to debate about which aspects are replicable—probably feelings of power, probably not hormonal changes—and whether its influence is meaningful. The argument concerns technicalities of study design and conduct, not the motives of any researcher, but the tone of the conversation has become heated. Some targets of the critics have dubbed them bullies and even terrorists. Cuddy has reported death threats. Psychology must engage in self-examination and improvement—for the sake of its future. The question is whether we can do it while minimizing polarization and psychological fallout for its practitioners.

[PEOPLE] WON'T WEAR
HITLER'S SWEATER EVEN
IF YOU'LL WASH IT AND
DO EVERYTHING YOU
CAN TO IT. IT ISN'T THE
PATHOGEN THREAT.
IT'S A MORAL THREAT.

98

PAUL ROZIN
b. 1936

SOURCE: The online interview "What Is Disgust?"
DATE: 2015
FIELD: Emotion

His online behavior sickens you, and her views are just revolting. Why is morality so bound up in the language of disgust? Paul Rozin is the master of that gross-out emotion, our deep evolutionary response to things that can sicken us, like rotting flesh or disease-carrying creatures. His colorful experiments show that disgust is very robust. Even if we know full well that the feces shape on the plate is chocolate, or the cockroach dipped in our juice was sterilized, we still find it difficult to partake in the snacks. It's not the rational antipathy to disease, it's that we can't stand the "essence" of cockroach.

These deep tendencies have been coopted over evolutionary time to be used against nonbodily offenses. Next time someone expresses disgust in a social context, note how their face changes. The nose wrinkles, and the nostrils close to keep bad smells away. The mouth flops open, sometimes with the tongue protruding, to push food out. We can still see the system for preventing physical contamination. Longstanding societal concepts like incest, or relatively recent offenders like Hitler, all provoke the response—now shorn of the bodily nausea but retaining the strong desire to shun and banish. Just like the essence of cockroach, a sweater can permanently hold the essence of Hitler. This work further confirms Hume's (see page 11) view of moral emotions, and gives it a deep evolutionary twist. We kept the rotten berries out of the mouths of our infants, and now we keep the corrupting influences out of the minds of our societies.

The mind is a difference-seeking machine.

The mind is a difference-seeking machine.

99

MAHZARIN BANAJI
b. 1956

SOURCE: The podcast *On Being*
DATE: 2016
FIELD: Perceptions and Biases

Mahzarin Banaji grew up in a minority group—as a Zoroastrian in India—and became a psychologist fascinated with the unconscious. She drew these influences together in the concept of implicit bias. These are stereotypes that we explicitly disavow but still carry under the surface. At projectimplicit.com you can explore these in a test, the Implicit Association Test (IAT). In the original race bias version, you categorize words as positive or negative, faces as black or white, using the same two keys. If you are slower when positive and black responses share the same key, this suggests bias. Banaji emphasizes implicit biases are difficult to eliminate, and don't make you a bad person: It's simply that the mind loves to form categories.

At the macro level, this research generates robust and interesting findings—researchers have used the method to produce racial bias maps for US states and the continent of Europe. However, the test isn't diagnostically precise enough to be used at an individual level, and nor is it clear that it can predict real-life prejudicial behavior. Banaji and the other test creators do not endorse such individual use, but implicit bias training, ubiquitous in many organizations, frequently uses the IAT as a diagnostic consciousness-raising tool, despite this. For other uses of the IAT, like for gender, the effects are harder to grasp. One version shows only a bias in women, with men unbiased. On another, women show more bias *against women* than men do. A lot of questions remain about what this test actually means, but it points to something vital about our difference-seeking minds.

MANY PEOPLE BELIEVE THAT MEMORY WORKS LIKE A RECORDING DEVICE [...] THAT JUST ISN'T TRUE. OUR MEMORIES ARE CONSTRUCTIVE. →

100

ELIZABETH LOFTUS
b. 1944

SOURCE: "How Can Our Memories Be Manipulated?", *TED Radio Hour*
DATE: 2017
FIELD: Memory

Elizabeth Loftus is the mistress of memory manipulation. She startled the field with her 1974 study showing people misremember the speed at which two cars collided, if you change the question to use the word "smashed" or "bumped" instead of "collided." Subsequent work suggested we can also fabricate memories: Participants remembered being lost in a mall, or meeting a figure at Disneyland, after being coached into thinking about the possibility.

Her motivations were partly personal; once a relative had almost mistakenly convinced her that, as a child, she was the one to discover her mother's dead body. She was also driven by skepticism about sexual abuse trials, where testimony was based on recovered childhood memories. She wanted to see whether trusted figures, such as therapists, could implant memories through directed questioning. This is obviously controversial, and Loftus has come under fire from therapists and people who report these sexual abuses. Other researchers argue that this research mainly shows the production of beliefs (I suppose I did...) rather than genuine memories. Yet Loftus has, by and large, stuck to her guns.

The recovered memory movement was driven by Freud's idea of repression, based largely on informal observations. More recently psychological scientists have shown evidence for directed forgetting that makes experiences harder to access in the future. This leaves science on both sides of the argument. Memories, or memory-like experiences, can be invented. Yet real memories can be driven underground. This leaves no definitive rule for approaching cases of remembered abuse, except to treat each on its merits.

INDEX

I Learned its rude To Call with or use

Its not in the Part of my Vernacular,
it at are brown man

CREDITS

There are lot of Inflections in dialect
It is a very Eclectic Word 'Ey'